T0128989

UNDER THEIR CLAWS

A TESTIMONY OF MY KIDNAPPING

by Myriam Norton

Order this book online at www.trafford.com
or email orders@trafford.com

Most Trafford titles are also available at major online book retailers.

Printed in the United States of America.

ISBN: 978-1-4669-0217-6 (sc)
ISBN: 978-1-4669-0218-3 (e)

Library of Congress Control Number: 2011919257

Trafford rev. 09/12/2012

 www.trafford.com

North America & international
toll-free: 1 888 232 4444 (USA & Canada)
phone: 250 383 6864 ♦ fax: 812 355 4082

THIS BOOK IS LOVINGLY DEDICATED
TO MY SONS, DAVID, ALEJANDRO AND
RICARDO, AND THEIR FAMILIES

———————————

WHEN YOU GET HOME TONIGHT
TAKE A MOMENT TO THINK OF THOSE
WHO ARE NOT AS FORTUNATE . . . THOSE
WHO REMAIN KIDNAPPED IN THE JUNGLES
OR THE FREEZING WILDERNESS
OF COLOMBIA.

———————————

PREFACE

ACCORDING TO STATISTICS, approximately 3,500 people were kidnapped every year in Colombia in the late 1990's and the first couple of years of the 2000's. This book was written between 2004 and 2008. Some of the political and social conditions may have changed by the time it is published. Although there were other groups carrying out abductions, the FARC guerrilla (Revolutionary Armed Forces of Colombia) is responsible for over two thirds of the total number of kidnappings that have occurred in Colombia.

A "Peace Treaty" between the Government and the FARC was taking place in a safe haven called "Zona de Distensión" at the time I was kidnapped. This area was granted to the FARC by President Pastrana, who hoped the government's concession to permit the FARC this large extension of land, where they could operate freely, would lead to an agreement and end the four and a half decades of guerrilla attacks, murders and kidnappings across the country. Ironically, while important officials came together around the "peace table", the FARC bandits were destroying small towns inhabited by innocent people. Some of the high ranking military officers were simultaneously jailed for "stepping over the line" when they tried to repel guerrilla attacks. As odd as it sounds, the Colombian Army was only allowed to fend off guerrillas AFTER they had assaulted a village, when it was already too late to prevent the killings and destruction. The army and police would chase the aggressors to the border line of the 'Zona de Distensión' but they weren´t allowed to step inside the FARC's safe haven.

It is common knowledge that all through the years, the FARC have had teams of spokesmen living in Europe who have done their best to convince idealistic individuals and mostly Non-Governmental Organizations that they are 'freedom fighters' struggling for the well-being of the down-trodden lower classes in Colombia. This went on until 9/11 when their actions were thoroughly investigated and at last, they were listed among the International Terrorist Groups. The truth is that previous to that time there was little understanding of the true nature of these alleged 'freedom fighters'. If they had true ideals for social justice at the birth of their movement, these had long since disappeared.

In the early nineties, the head of the Medellin Drug Cartel, Pablo Escobar, along with the leaders of other drug cartels, were either killed or put in jail. The FARC took over a large sector of the cocaine business. Much of their income came from the thirty percent 'taxes' collected from the coca-leaf growers, processors, distributors and local buyers. Adding these 'taxes' to the enormous amounts of money they collected from their kidnapping 'industry', the FARC became the richest terrorist group in the world.

There was an increase in the number of abductions and other types of violence in Colombia that caused thousands of respectable people, mainly business owners that generated employment for middle and low-income employees, to leave the country. This caused a shift in living conditions, reducing many middle-income families to poverty and crushing the low-income population into misery. Progress was stunted and poverty became as prevalent as it had been several decades earlier. Colombia, a beautiful country full of good-natured people, has endured this state of terrorism for close to half a century. My abduction was similar to most other kidnappings of a single, common person. Unfortunately, other Latin American countries are now being contaminated by this abominable crime.

FOREWORD

By General Alvaro Valencia Tovar
Colombian Army (retired)

ABDUCTION IS ONE of the most vicious crimes ever conceived by the human mind. The torture of a defenseless victim is compounded by the anguish caused to his or her family. The Revolutionary Armed Forces of Colombia (FARC) have been using this damnable crime for over four decades as a financial source and a tool to obtain political dividends for their declared war against the constitutional Colombian Government.

The main objective of the FARC, the terrorist group guilty of approximately seventy percent of the kidnappings in Colombia, is to pervert the minds and harden the hearts of young Colombian peasants through a form of political indoctrination, a remnant of the former Marxist ideology. This helps to explain their cruel and harsh treatment of the kidnapped people. It has become an arrogant display of wickedness that manifests the evolution of formerly good-natured country people into sadistic monsters. Drug dealing, the core of Colombia's present situation, is the main source of financial income for the so called guerrillas. It is not only a Colombian concern, but a worldwide problem that deserves urgent attention. Drug consumption is the most dangerous threat to our world's youngsters, a menace that cannot be defeated by one solitary country. What is required is a true political, judicial, and military alliance that will take joint action against the six stages of this gigantic, criminal business: cultivation, manufacture, exportation, distribution, consumption and money laundering.

Myriam Norton's deeply moving book is the shocking account of her own abduction. The culprits were an armed band of that terrorist organization, whose goal was to obtain a 'juicy' ransom from her family.

Coming from a socially affluent environment that afforded her a peaceful, cultured way of life, this European-born lady suddenly had to face unexpected, harsh treatment brutally imposed upon her by a gang of former Communist guerrillas turned into drug-dealing terrorists and common bandits. How could an elderly, educated lady survive and retain her psychological balance? The answer reveals the positive side of the drama. In Myriam's own words, "Chaotic situations bring out the best in people." The captivity and hardships experienced by the hostages helped them develop a degree of togetherness and mutual support that probably would not have occurred under normal circumstances.

The powerful source of Myriam´s fortitude was the constant presence of God and she often asked for the help of that Superior Force, who oversees human events. Even small happenings, such as finding a half-torn book in the mud, motivated a heartfelt expression of gratitude to her Lord, who kept her spirits rather high throughout her challenging ordeal.

The author vividly describes her riveting experience in this book. It is a blend of emotion and physical pain. And despite the horror of her circumstances, her sense of humor, inner courage and above all, her powerful instinct of self-preservation made it possible for her to endure.

Myriam's account of the criminal side of the guerrillas is not merely the story of a dreadful personal experience, but when the reader finishes the last page of the book, he will feel concern for the thousands of lives that are affected by the savage FARC kidnappers. Colombian readers will appreciate this lady for her priceless contribution to exposing the reality of the FARC guerrillas, who skillfully disguise themselves to fool the world and to cover their criminal behavior.

INTRODUCTION

THIS IS THE chronicle of a unique experience that marked my life forever. It is the true story of my painful ordeal of being kidnapped by the FARC (Revolutionary Armed Forces of Colombia), in April 2003.

Kidnapping has been a torment to Colombian society for over half a century. Most of the victims are hard-working, ordinary people, whose families end up steeped in debt after paying the ransom. There is little chance to save a victim's life if his family, or the company he works for, refuses to pay. Furthermore, if the FARC bandits believe there is some money left in the family coffers after paying the ransom, they often abduct another one of its members, or even their original victim, a second time.

My memoir includes, in detail, the sub-human living conditions we captives had to endure and the way such deprivation affected us. After my release, my son Alejandro, a psychiatrist who lives in the United States, suggested that my healing process would be accelerated if I wrote down my thoughts and experiences when I had bouts of insomnia due to the bad memories. We went over the notes together the next day. With his help, I was able to find closure through my catharsis. This book is the result of my notes. My story is true to life, and not exaggerated in any way. For security reasons, some names and dates had to be changed.

It wasn't my intention to write a book, and I had no access to a pen or paper, not even the light of a candle. If I had known I would be documenting my experience, I would have tried to make more contact with some of the 'guerilleros', although this was something we hostages tried to avoid. At that time, my priority was focused on survival and maintaining my sanity.

I decided to write my memoir in English instead of Spanish, my first language, because I want people everywhere to know what the FARC guerillas are doing to Colombia. Abduction is such a wide-spread crime that most Colombians have a relative or a friend who has suffered this ordeal.

Another reason for having it published in English, abroad, is the concern that making my document known in Colombia could endanger my family. The guerrillas consider people in the media 'military targets' and many have been murdered. This explains why some that wrote about their kidnappings had to flee the country when their writings came to light. I changed a few names, places and dates, for security reasons.

Despite the risk, I feel it´s important to share my experience. I am sure that in other parts of the world, the subject will be unusual and interesting and my hope is to spread the word by creating more awareness as to this primitive practice.

Though it was a sore subject for him, my son, David, told me in detail about the process that he, and a committee of five friends, followed to negotiate my freedom. He made me promise I would never ask how much he and his brothers paid to save my life; they agreed that I should never know.

I wasn't born in Colombia and yet I feel deeply connected to, and a part of, this beautiful country where my family immigrated when I was only six months old. Bogotá, the capital, has always been my home—the birthplace of my children and most of my grandchildren. Like most folks, before my kidnapping I was a silent witness to the events that have weakened the country and its society. Poverty existed before, but it was tremendously increased by so many years of continued violence. While I am writing, over two million people are jobless and thousands of families have been left homeless.

I consider myself blessed to be alive, free, and capable of speaking out. Scores of others didn't survive or have been permanently, physically or emotionally incapacitated.

If you want to know how an elderly woman feels being 'merchandise' in the hands of such bandits, let me take you on a trip to a FARC 'retention camp' on a barren, cold, moor of the Andes.

Elevation:	Approx. 13.000 feet above sea-level.
Temperature:	30—40 degrees Fahrenheit
Weather:	Fog and drizzle every day

Because of the high altitude, the sun's rays burnt harshly when we had a few, sporadic hours of sunshine. The drizzle, rain and wind whipped us cruelly the rest of the time.

ACKNOWLEDGEMENTS

My first words of thankfulness go out to my dear friends, Jaime and Julio, in recognition of their courageous action in my favor.

I want to express my deep gratitude to the six wonderful people on my rescue 'Comité' (Committee). Their kindness, hours of hard work and dedication brought me back to life. These dedicated volunteers spent the months I was kidnapped helping David plan every step, down to the last detail, so he could successfully negotiate with the terrorists until they finally achieved my release. May God always bless them.

My sincere admiration and gratitude goes out to my dear friends, Irene and Gary, who spent endless hours working with me on my manuscript. Their enthusiasm and invaluable help made this book possible. They asked many questions about the abominable conditions we lived in that helped me to focus on details, bringing to life the surroundings just as they were. Their unconditional support has been precious to me.

Irene and her husband, Santiago, are missionaries and directors of a Foundation dedicated to teenagers-at-risk in the poorest neighborhoods of Bogotá. They lead an inspiring program of workshops where they teach young people values and attitudes towards life: honesty, compassion, forgiveness, and how to strive for peace in their country. Several years have passed, and my book has been edited thoroughly. Irene has helped me up until the end and we have a wonderful, everlasting friendship.

I also extend my thanks to my long standing friend, General Alvaro Valencia Tovar, a renowned Colombian historian and retired General. It is an honor to me that he enthusiastically wrote my foreword, the epilogue, and revised the historical data for accuracy. General Valencia is certainly one of the most respected people in the country and was a candidate for the Presidency of Colombia in l978. He is frequently consulted by U. S. officials on Colombia's political situation.

My friend Dianne worked long hours with me in Florida and her gift of asking questions enriched my story with personal data I wouldn´t have remembered otherwise. I will always cherish her warm and caring friendship.

A special thanks to my editor, Phyllis Dolislager, an author and literary consultant. Her contribution served to improve my writing at its ending stages and she offered important suggestions to change the structure of my project. She turned a difficult task into something enjoyable.

UNDER THEIR CLAWS

Chapter 1

THAT FATEFUL DAY

AT LAST I was back at my farm breathing in the aroma of the fertile earth and the fragrant air. For many years I had scraped this rich soil out from under my fingernails after laboring to nurse the plants in their first stages of life. I couldn't wait to inspect our latest experiment, the guanábana trees, in bloom for the first time. As usual, Jaider, the caretaker, was by my side.

Suddenly, I felt the shocking sensation of two cold, iron objects pressed against my temples. I froze.

"Oh, my God! Could these be . . . ? ? ? ? ? ?"

My head was pounding as my worst fears descended upon me. I squinted at the glare of sunlight bouncing off the shiny revolver barrels tightly gripped in the dirty hands of two gruesome looking men. It happened so quickly that all I can remember is the terrifying thought of death being but an instant away. My arms were trapped in the sturdy grips of my assailants, and I had no choice but to follow their orders.

"The 'patrón' wants ya in the house", one of them growled. My heart sank deeper as we reached the living-room where two other men were pointing guns at Nydia, (Jaider's wife) their three children, my driver Rodrigo, and another worker.

"Ya better not put up a fight and come with us or I'll kill'em here n'now," one of them threatened in a blood-chilling tone. He was a strange, ugly man with dark, ominous circles under his eyes and a cold, morose face.

Mustering up all my courage I answered, "I'll go with you, but please don't hurt them." Then I heard myself asking where they were going to take me.

He gave me the same answer, "Ya better hurry—the patron don't like ta wait. We'll bring ya back this afternoon".

"Is this a kidnapping"? I asked.

"No, are ya deaf? Ya'll be back tanight. We're even gonna' go in yar car. Where'ya been? Ya ain't been 'round for five weeks. We've been waitin' around n'checking you out—ya ain't easy ta find."

If they knew I hadn't been there lately, what else did they know? One of them pulled a bottle out of his pocket while the other grabbed my hair, yanked my head back, and forced a greenish liquid down my throat. I fought to spit it out, so he pointed his gun at my head again and made me gulp it down. It was oh, so bitter! It must have been the famous 'Burundanga', a narcotic known to cause paralysis of the brain if taken in excess. My eyes met with stares of horror on the faces of my workers as I was dragged away. Two men stayed behind—one held them at gunpoint while the other tied them up.

The man with the dark circles under his eyes demanded my ID card and the car's registration papers. He grabbed my purse and pushed me into the back of my faithful, old, Peugeot truck that had transported me to and from the farm for many years. My shock was so intense that it didn't occur to me this was the last time I would lay eyes on my beloved 'finca'(farm); a nesting place for my young ones and a source of many wonderful family memories.

Another man took the wheel and drove roughly to the gate, where he stopped to pick up two people waiting in a parked car at the side of the road. They were a strange pair; one was a woman and the other, a bizarre-looking specimen with long hair and a strong, muscular body that was absurdly out of place in a mini-skirt, leotards and make-up caked thickly over 'his' face. Was I hallucinating?

There were rumors that the FARC were demanding a monthly 'vacuna' (vaccine), a nicer name for extortion, from two rich cattle ranchers nearby. These were the only FARC encounters I had heard of in the region.

The man at the wheel was a terrible driver and couldn't keep my truck under control. Between curses, he tried to pick up speed in first gear, forcing the clutch so hard, the car broke down. They simply dumped it by the side of the road and dragged me to another vehicle following close behind. By that time everything was hazy and I was seeing double. The rest of the day was lost to me. I must have lapsed in and out of consciousness, completely unaware of my whereabouts. Later, I found out that my abductors were common criminals, who carried out the actual abduction, and then sold their victim to the FARC.

*   *   *   *   *   *

We lived in Bogotá, the capital, and spent many week-ends at our second home, 'Buganviles', two hours from the city. Although I longed to be there, lately I had stayed away as much as possible in respect for my son's concern about my security. As painful as it was, we were considering selling.

It was practically impossible to sell a farm in Colombia at that time, so I grasped at the opportunity to exchange ours for a small condominium in Bogotá. The realtor arranged a meeting with prospective clients for the following Saturday.

On Tuesday, Rodrigo picked me up at my apartment, early in the morning. I had trained him to handle my commercial activities, buy fertilizers, sell the produce, and collect payments from the clients. He represented me to the best of his ability in all issues pertaining to the farm's productivity. Nevertheless, even with his help, it would take some work to get everything in perfect condition for the client's visit after five weeks of my absence.

Beautiful azaleas, hydrangeas, hibiscus in all colors, and other tropical plants that flourish all year round, greeted us as we approached the house. It was exciting to see my 'guanábana' trees first bloom. I knew the tilapias (a species of fish native to the area) were breeding in the lake, and the entire property was buzzing with the lushness that characterizes the Colombian countryside. Yet, I was haunted by the sad feeling that our farm would soon belong to someone else. My abduction froze the transaction and it never came about.

Chapter 2

WAKING UP TO REALITY

My urgent need to relieve myself woke me in the middle of the night. I was still groggy, but aware enough to realize that I was in a wooden hut, lying on a burlap sack on a dirt floor and covered with only a tiny blanket. A dim, overhead light-bulb cast a somber shadow on the shabby room and I could hear the sound of mice nibbling on something very close to me. And it was so terribly cold!

I stood up with difficulty and tried to open the door—it was locked from the outside. I knocked. A guard in a camouflaged uniform showed me to a filthy toilet. As he escorted me back, I noticed there were two other men standing guard outside the door. "Where am I?" I asked, before he could lock me up again. One of them muttered, "The boss'l tell ya in the mornin."

I fell back down on the burlap sack. Was there any chance my vague memories from the day before were only nightmares? Was I going to wake up and find myself safely back in my bed at home? The more my thoughts cleared, the more my hopes dwindled and the hopelessness of the situation began to sink in.

"My God, is this real?" I slowly relived the gruesome happenings from the beginning and all evidence indicated that I should suspect the worst. Nevertheless, the words of the first bandit, "Ya'll be back t'night", had me clinging to the faint hope that what I feared wasn't true. The chill grew deeper and deeper. I remembered telling 'Mutti' (German for Mom) that I'd be back in Bogotá around four pm the previous day. She must have been beside herself by now.

In Bogotá, I usually wore a thermal undershirt for protection from the cool climate; but now I was dressed for Buganviles, in a very light, sweat suit. The woolen sweater I always took along for my return trip wasn't anywhere to be seen. To my dismay, when I glanced down at my hand, I saw that the antique diamond ring, my parents' gift on my fifteenth birthday, was gone.

On my second trip to the bathroom, I became aware that the cabin was filling up with boys and girls dressed in camouflaged military uniforms. They were all heavily armed teenagers, with machine guns and bullet-belts strapped across their chests. Some appeared to be only a few years older than my grandchildren. I was hopelessly surrounded by very dangerous strangers who had the power to kill me at a moment's notice.

My anguish grew so intense that I could barely function. Tears were flowing in torrents and my only two Kleenex tissues were soaked. I hung them up to dry on a string dangling between two wooden walls.

It was still dark when someone brought me a little pot of rice soup and an 'arepa', (a round, flat, corn tart). I was famished and devoured it immediately. Another man brusquely opened the door and ordered me to get ready for my trip to the 'campamento'(camp). He told me it would take two to three days on horse-back, or about five to six days on foot, and we were leaving immediately. When I asked to speak to his boss, he assured me the 'comandante' would come soon.

He stared at me wildly as he locked me in and shouted, "Está-Secuestrada! . . . Está Secuestrada . . . secues . . . secuestrada!" . . . Ya're kidnapped, . . . ya're kidnapped . . . kid . . . kidnapped, . . . ya're . . . kidnapped . . . secuestrada . . . kid secues . . . trada . . . trada . . . kidnapped . . . napped . . . kid . . . napped . . . trada . . . kid . . . secuestrada . . . secues . . . napped . . . napped . . . secues . . . kid . . . trada . . . secues . . . napped echoed in my mind. It's impossible to describe the crushing impact of those words. They robbed me of any hope I would awake from the nightmare and a wave of bleakness and total misery swept over me.

Soon, another dark, middle-aged fellow, who I assumed was the 'comandante', burst into the room. Facing him with all my strength I asked, "Who are you?"

"We are the FARC," he proudly announced.

"Is this a . . . kidnapping?"

"No, it's only an 'economic retention'."

"Why me?" I asked trying to stay calm.

"Ya're a rich woman and the FARC needs money to support the cause. We know'bout yar house and yar farm," He smirked.

In a shaky attempt to reason with him I said,

"I'm not wealthy. Surely I'll be nothing but a burden to you with my heart trouble and osteoarthritis in my hands."

"No prablem," he said, heartlessly, "we can take one'a ya sons instead. All ya have t'do is tell us where'da find him—we'll bring'im in for an exchange and send ya home in a few days".

Did he really think I was going to expose one of my sons to this hellish situation? My anguish turned into burning rage. "His mother would probably accept such an offer. That explains why he is the beast that he is!" I thought to myself. Once the rage began to burn, it didn't stop.

He left the room abruptly and soon a female 'guerrillera' came in with paper and pen and told me to write down any medicine I needed. She assured me the 'comandante' would send for it at once.

Nervously, I made my list of prescription medicine for high blood pressure and osteoarthritis, vitamins and a few other essentials such as sunscreen and nose drops. Crying stuffs up noses and I had a feeling there would be much more of it up ahead. I couldn´t expect my usual Lancôme creams so I added Ponds to the list.

The guerrillas weren´t going to risk being followed by the army and were in a hurry to get going. I had to act quickly. I folded the little blanket lengthwise, crossed it over my shoulder, and stuffed it under my sweat-shirt. Then I tucked one point into the waistband at the front of my slacks, and the other in the back.

They gave me a very light, unlined red jacket with a hood and a zipper down the front. It was certainly no match for the bone-chilling cold but better than nothing.

Meanwhile: Back at the farm

After I was forced to drink the greenish liquid and dragged away by the bandits, they abandoned the premises. Rodrigo and Jaider managed to free themselves and untie the others. They ran to the road and caught the first bus to Anapoima, the nearest town, where they reported my kidnapping to the Police and called my son, Ricardo.

A few minutes earlier, before I arrived at our farm, my son Ricardo called me on my cell-phone and told me he felt uneasy about my being there. But he knew my trip was necessary to get the house ready for our client's visit and it would be impossible to dissuade me. He wished me luck. We agreed to spend a short vacation together as soon as the deal was signed.

Ricardo went into shock when he heard Jaider's news. His wife, Doris, was finally able to calm him down enough to call my other son, Alejandro, in the United States, and Hernando, their father. They agreed to meet the next evening in Bogotá.

Early next morning the anti-kidnapping squad arrived at the farm and interviewed everyone who had been present during the incident. My sons were then informed that some of their answers were incoherent and contradictory.

Chapter 3

THE JOURNEY

The old, one-eyed horse was for me. My captors weren´t concerned if I knew how to ride or not, they were only interested in getting me to my destination as soon as possible. A young 'guerillero,' carrying his shotgun and wearing a band of bullets across his chest, led my horse by the halter. We started slowly up a very steep and narrow trail that skirted the mountainside, with a precipice on the right. Another fellow walked behind. I could only see about four or five feet ahead through the dense fog. The relentless, biting wind and permanent drizzle only made things worse. My anxiety grew when I realized the horse's empty eye-socket was on the same side as the precipice. I had no control over the horse because the young guy was leading him by the halter. I hadn't been on horseback for at least forty years.

"What's your name?" I asked the boy.

"Francisco".

"How old are you?"

"Eighteen."

He couldn't have been a day older than thirteen, but the FARC refuse to admit they have children in their ranks.

The majestic, Andes mountain-range crosses Colombia from South to North. When the fog eased up, I saw that I was surrounded by endless rows of peaks spread out on all sides, separating me from everything I loved. My sense of direction dissolved in the maze of slopes and trails as we climbed and descended those mountains, and the distance between us and any kind of civilization grew wider and wider with every step. Vertigo kept me from looking over the cliffs and prayer came easily.

A flat rock partially blocking the path loomed up in front of us. Even though there was enough room to pass around it, Francisco forced the poor horse to scramble over it. His brusqueness added to my growing anxiety as I rocked back and forth on the old horse´s back while it slipped and struggled to keep its balance. There was usually a river or a brook we had to cross at the foot of each mountain and I got soaked up to my waist several times. Once, I feared I would be swept away when we had to cross a deep river and its icy water came up to my neck. Fortunately, the old horse's judgment was better than I expected, and we reached the other side.

It was raining most of the time. The sun appeared at intervals and shone so brightly that I was sunburned before the rain started up again. One by one, we climbed every muddy, slippery mountain trail and descended the steep slope on the other side. I held on to the saddle-horn for dear life as we ascended, and then grabbed on to an opening in the back of the saddle as we descended. The impressive and yet desolate mountain range was endless and I felt so tiny and frightened! There was no sign of life to be seen—not a house, a person, or even an animal. Many hours passed when I asked Francisco if we were getting near our destination.

His answer was, "We might git there ba tamorrow night—that's if ya're lucky and don't break yar neck. If ya do break it and stop walkin´, we'll just leave ya and tell the boss that the 'merchandise' croaked on us!"

At one point, Francisco violently beat the horse and yanked the rope. It tried to find its footing, but tripped and fell. I slipped off just in time to prevent the full weight of its body from crushing me. Francisco was succeeding with his sadistic plan. Soon I had a huge, painful, bruise on my left calf. I begged him not to do this again, but when we reached the next group of rocks he beat the horse so brutally that it jumped and we fell again. Amazingly, even though I was sore and bruised all over, I didn't seem to have a fracture.

At eight p.m. we arrived at a little adobe house, the home of a peasant couple with their three small children, and an elderly man. They were friendly and reminded me of my 'campesino' (farmer) friends near our country house. Carlota, the wife, gave me a pajama and wool socks to wear while she washed my underclothes, scraped the caked dirt off my outer clothes, and hung them to dry over the stove.

As I sat by the warmth of the stove, my thoughts drifted back to my family. Certainly, by this time Rodrigo and Jaider must have notified my son, Ricardo, of my misfortune and he would have told the others. David, the eldest, was in Hong Kong on a business trip, and my other son, Alejandro, lives in the United States. Would my poor Mutti (mother), who was 92 at the time, live through this? Both she and I were going to have to find the strength to survive if we were to see each other again. Would I return to my loved ones? There was a constant, lurking, dark thought reminding me that many kidnapped people never return. It was always there, coming and going in the back of my mind.

Carlota brought me some rice, a chicken wing and potatoes and invited me to watch TV in the room where they slept with their children. There was a tiny room with two beds. One of them was for their 'occasional visitors', and the other was occupied by her father. Before we slept that night, I told the old man about my abduction. A look of compassion crossed his face.

"Mi señora, we're ashamed to be involved but we have no choice. We don't approve of the FARC's actions, but we have nowhere else to live. They've taken over the whole region." He shifted uncomfortably.

"What do you know about these people?"

He paused as he carefully weighed his words,

"I knew Tirofijo (the FARC leader) as a child. He watched his parents being murdered during the 'Violencia' (a period of intense, political conflict and brutality in the 40's and 50's). When he was old enough, he rounded up other young 'campesinos' (peasants) to take revenge. They say they follow the Communist ideals of a fellow called Marx, but frankly, between you and me, they're just a bunch of heartless criminals."

He continued, "When the Soviet Union fell, and the FARC lost Cuba's support, they turned to kidnappings and drug traffic. Our governments have put up with the guerrillas for too many years. They should have been stopped at the beginning. We Colombians don't stand up for our rights—just take a look at our 'compadres' in Ecuador, who just kicked out their useless president."

"A Peace Treaty was signed in the early eighties when the FARC organized the Unión Patriótica (UP) as their political party. Their candidate, Jaime Pardo Leal, was soon murdered. Some groups on both sides refused to respect the treaty. FARC units kept up the kidnappings, while vengeful relatives killed most of the UP's political leaders who wanted to return to normal life." He had dignity and an air of wisdom.

"What do you think they'll do to me?"

"They'll call your family to make their demand, and will only let you go after they receive the ransom. They always start out demanding enormous sums, usually in dollars, but they'll slowly negotiate, accepting a lower sum in the end, in pesos. They know exactly what properties you own because they have people infiltrated in the banks and income-tax offices who keep them informed. Is your family very rich?"

"No, we're well to do, but not rich. We all work hard to make a living. My sons are young professionals beginning their careers and raising families of their own." The conversation changed course and I dozed off to sleep. This was my last night in a bed.

It was still dark when Carlota woke me up to a substantial breakfast: two fried eggs, an 'arepa' (flat corn tart), hot chocolate and a big bowl of potato soup.

"Dear, you should try to eat as much as you can because you won't get anything else for the rest of the day. It'll be a tough journey," she told me.

But who could eat all that food at 5:00 a.m., especially under so much stress? I made an effort to force part of it down.

As soon as we were left alone for a moment Carlota told me, "I'm so sorry you're going through this, and Dear, I'll pray to my "Virgencita de Chiquiquinquirá" (little Virgin of a town called Chiquinquirá) to protect you. They often bring kidnapped people here to pass the night on their way to and from the camps. It always makes me cry to see how sick and squalid they are when they return. When they keep them for a long time—like several years, they are usually out of their minds. But my "Virgencita" (she showed me her little statue), won't let this happen to you. She'll get you out real fast—even less than a year—and she'll make you very patient. Sancho and I don't like what the FARC are doing to you people but our little farm is here, in their territory, so we have to follow their orders, or else . . ."

At 6 a.m., two men wearing straw hats, jeans and 'ruanas' (woolen ponchos) approached the house on horseback. They were to be my escorts for the next leg of the journey. Immediately, I sensed the difference between these men and the guerilleros of the day before. Mario and Edwin weren't hostile and if they were armed, they didn't display it.

Reluctantly, I climbed onto the horse and turned to say goodbye. Carlota waved sadly from the door of her cabin. This time, my horse was not pulled by the halter, but walked between theirs´. The trip was longer but it seemed less harrowing because we stopped every two hours to rest our knees. Mario told me the water in the brooks was clean enough to drink; it was gratifying to quench our thirst along the way. Crossing the rivers on horseback was always frightening, especially when the horses stumbled in the holes in the river bed and struggled to come up again. We crossed three rivers and climbed one mountain after another. I was soaked to the bone and shivering intensely.

While we were riding, I recalled a haunting incident a friend told me about only a few months before my capture. One of her aunts was in her late seventies; appealing prey for the FARC because her sons owned a chain of stores. They strapped the poor woman to the saddle and tied the horse to a cable stretched between two mountains. The horse was pulled across the gorge or canyon by a pulley system, suspended in thin air. This terrifying and deadly form of transportation is called a 'tarabita'. After twenty months of abduction, the lady was finally released when the family paid an enormous ransom. She died a week later.

I asked Mario and Edwin if something like this was awaiting me. They assured me that after many accidents, the FARC stopped using these shortcuts to transport their 'merchandise'. It wasn't to their advantage to lose me on the way.

Not far into our journey, we passed through a beautiful rain forest of native trees adorned with colourful, wild flowers, thick moss and a large variety of ferns. Never before had I seen such a breath taking, natural garden. The sight of it moved me to tears and a desperate prayer welled up in my soul.

We soon reached a stretch of brown sludge indicating the bare beginnings of a badly engineered mountain road. We were forced to travel on and off the trail to keep the horses safe. At one point, my horse's legs were buried so deep in the mud that it couldn't move. To my horror, while I was sitting on it, Mario beat it brutally until it reacted and climbed out of the mud. This was the only way to save it from certain death.

At about 2 p.m. we stopped at a wooden house full of 'guerrilleros'. It was bizarre and shocking to see three very young girls, not older than eleven or twelve, clad in tiny camouflaged uniforms, sitting on the laps of middle-aged men that touched them in an abusive manner.

We still had a long way to go to reach our destination before nightfall and I was making an effort not to think about what was up ahead.

At around five thirty p.m. we looked down and there, on the lower ridge of the mountain, was a large group of camouflaged tents.

Edwin explained that this was where the 'Comandantes' lived. These important FARC leaders were not to be seen by outsiders so we couldn´t approach the 'Compañia'. Mario ran down the slope towards the tents and returned with two 'guerrilleros', assigned to "officially deliver the 'merchandise'" to the camp I was assigned to.

When we were alone, Edwin made his humble confession, "You're a nice lady—you don't deserve this. If the territory we live on wasn't under the FARC'S control, things would be different. We have no choice!" He raised his hand up and made the motion of slashing his throat.

"I advise you not to try to escape. You wouldn't have a chance making it back alive by yourself." I wished them well and they rode away.

The idea of escaping had crossed my mind, but I knew that trying to find my way out of that 'páramo' (freezing, mountain-range) would be hopeless.

Two, new teen-age 'guerrilleros' were there to guide me to the camp. I was in the hands of uncouth youngsters that didn't have a notion about how to treat a human being. After several hours, one of them told me we were getting close to our journey's end. He seemed to think it was nice place to live and referred to it as "a cool camp".

We came to another river, much wider and deeper than the others. They wanted me to cross it by myself but I was afraid of the strong current and depth of the water. If I had barely crossed the smaller rivers, how would I fare with this one? I asked one of them to please lead my horse to the other side; he did. My horse slipped several times and lost its balance, plunging me into the deep water. It was truly miraculous that I was able to hold on to the saddle and didn't catch pneumonia after being completely soaked in the icy water and unable to change into dry clothes during those two, dreadful days. By the time I reached the other side, I was shivering violently and every bone and muscle in my body hurt.

We continued traveling along the border of another mountain until we reached a small, rustic, wooden shack. The night was dark and gloomy, and there was no light anywhere, not even the flicker of a gas lantern in the distance.

MEANWHILE, IN BOGOTÁ: DAY 3

My sons, Alejandro, and Ricardo, traveled to Bogotá to meet with their father, Hernando. It took David two days to return from his business trip in Hong Kong.

The next morning they reported the incident at the 'Gaula', the official Anti-Kidnapping Police Headquarters in Bogotá. They were told a search unit would be sent out on a special operation in an attempt to locate me before the bandits had a chance to take me, either far up on the 'páramo' (cold, mountain wilderness), or to the jungle, where they have most of their 'retention camps'. They knew that time was short and it would take the kidnappers five to six days by foot, or about three days on horseback to transport me far enough out of reach where I couldn't be found. Despite the possible risk, my anguished sons had to sign a statement authorizing the Army to carry out a military operation for my rescue. They were advised that, if they didn't find me within a week, it would be safer to go through the long and stressful negotiation process and pay the ransom as soon as an agreement was reached.

They explained that the reason for most kidnappings is to collect a ransom. The only way for a kidnapped victim's life to be saved is for the family to successfully negotiate with the FARC and come to a direct agreement with them as to the sum. Trying to avoid payment altogether would be too risky.

Alejandro contacted a friend who had been kidnapped and released after eight months. His family successfully negotiated his freedom and the FARC let him go after they collected the ransom. He was more than willing to help, and introduced Alejandro to Captain Pérez, a retired Army officer who had conducted the safe return of three other kidnapped victims over the past year. Captain Perez advised my sons to set up a committee of five or six people, immediately, who would meet every day to plan the negotiation strategy.

Chapter 4

MY FIRST THIRTY YEARS

IT WAS A crucial time in Vienna—the threat of war permeated the atmosphere. Hitler had announced his fatal plan to create a superior race and things looked sombre. My parents, a young Jewish couple, left everything behind, crossing the ocean to escape the Holocaust. Our family arrived in Colombia with grateful hearts, prepared to start a new life. I was six months old.

The Colombian Consul in Vienna and his wife were neighbours to my parents, and they became close friends. When they were planning to return to their country, they encouraged my parents to leave Vienna and move to Bogotá. This friendship marked our destiny.

We were a small family; my Dad (Vatti), a young lawyer; my mother (Mutti), the manager of my grandparents' silk boutiques in Vienna; my four-year old brother Martin, and me.

Vatti immediately went to work arranging the paperwork for our trip, but things were getting more and more dangerous. One of my uncles, a doctor, managed to hospitalize Vatti for a few days to hide him from the Nazis until everything was organized. Mutti took us to a farm in the country where we waited for Vatti, and after much suspense, he arrived. The timing worked out to perfection and we were able to catch a ship to Colombia. Only a small minority of Jewish families managed to escape compared to the vast numbers that were annihilated. We were among them.

My maternal grandmother, Omi, was not allowed to leave Austria with us. Vatti must have moved heaven and earth to help her, because after three years, right in the middle of the war, she was able to join us in Colombia. I ignore the details of her story because I was very small when she came and it was a rule in the family not to bring up the unpleasant memories of the past.

There was much sadness when my parents lost contact with my aunt Vally, her husband and small son who were imprisoned in a concentration camp.

*   *   *   *   *   *

When we arrived in Bogotá, the population was under 400,000 and good working opportunities abounded for anyone who had an education. It wasn't easy for my parents to start from scratch. They weren't Spanish speakers and had to become familiar with the customs of this exotic and unique land. But they were young, bright and quick learners. Vatti had to find a job immediately to support the family, leaving him no time to study for a Colombian legal license. Fortunately, he spoke English and was soon hired to represent an American hardware company that he worked for the rest of his life. He was a kind, friendly and hardworking young man, and he fit well into any social group.

At first, Vatti had to travel all over Colombia in old buses on bumpy, curvy roads sleeping in cheap, run-down hotels. After several rough years, my parents began to enjoy a more comfortable lifestyle, and established life-long friendships with Colombian, European and American couples. When we visited other cities we were often invited to his clients´ homes.

We spoke German at home, and I grew up speaking both languages. For my tenth birthday, my parents took me to New York on a two month vacation to visit my paternal grandparents. This was a great opportunity to pick up the English language. On our return to Bogotá I was enrolled in a bilingual, Spanish-English school.

My grandmother, Omi, was a courageous woman who had raised her three children all alone after her young husband died. Her friendliness and pleasant disposition won everyone's approval. Even though she never learned to speak Spanish very well, she always made herself understood. Omi and I spent much time together and she was a strong influence in my life. She walked me to school every day, taught me to pray, to bake cookies, to knit, embroider, play cards and more. She accompanied me to my ballet classes and was embarrassingly proud of my progress. She never approved my habit of whistling which she considered unladylike. She used to tell me: "Maedeln die pfeifen und Haehnen die kraehen, soll man bei Zeiten die Haelse umdrehen". (Girls that whistle and hens that crow, should sometimes have their necks rung in a battle.)

I was a happy and privileged child, frequently admired for my dark curly hair, green eyes and happy disposition. My parents', like most marriages, wasn't perfect but they were careful not to burden us with their problems. I can't remember ever having been lonely or neglected. They passed on to us a love for life and its splendor, in so many ways.

Vatti used to tell us, "A book is always a friend; you'll never be lonely if you have something interesting to read." We went to every concert and theatrical performance available in Bogotá which gave both my brother and I a taste for classical music and theater.

My parents knew how important it was to expose us to the pleasure of traveling, the enjoyment of meeting people and the acceptance of other cultures. Every vacation, no matter how short, took us to a different area of Colombia. This taught Martin and me to admire the beauty of nature, and every other year we traveled either to the United States or to one of the neighboring South American countries.

As soon as my parents felt comfortable with the Spanish language and could afford the fees, we joined the Bogotá Country Club. Now, we enjoyed other activities such as tennis, horseback excursions, and my favorite sport; swimming. I took it very seriously and joined the swimming team. My dad took me to intensive training every morning and evening at the Club pool, and I successfully participated in all the open, local swimming championships. At fifteen, I won the adult breast-stroke title in the State of Cundinamarca Swimming Championship and soon, I was filling our mantelpiece with silver trophies. But being Austrian, I was not allowed to participate in the Colombian National Swimming Championship.

My teen-age years were unforgettable. I was outgoing and spirited and would not be easily intimidated. Dancing was one of my favorite pastimes—'Domingos Bailables para Coca-Colos,' (Sunday dances for teenagers) at the Country Club were the highlight of the week. At the age of seventeen, my graduation present was a trip to Europe with Mutti on the Reina del Mar, a British ocean liner. It was important for me to come in touch with my European heritage and that trip made a memorable impact. Vatti and Omi had decided never to return to Vienna and Martin was studying at Princeton.

Two months after returning from Europe I traveled to the United States to study at Bryant College, a business school. It was time to leave my childhood behind and live, for the first time, away from home. There were twenty two girls in my dorm and Mrs. Evans, our housemother. Being the only foreigner, I was often invited to my friends' homes over the week-ends and my social life expanded.

My easy-going personality helped me adapt quickly. I was serious about my studies while I also made new friends. Soon, I began to date, learned to do the Jitter-bug, and taught my friends the Latin-American dances. It was nice to be around the girls, and still nicer to be surrounded by boys. Fortunately, my conservative up-bringing kept me from getting into trouble.

*   *   *   *   *   *

After graduating from College, I returned to Bogotá to live with my family. On that same week I was hired to be the interpreter and bilingual secretary to the Agricultural Attaché at the American Embassy. I loved my job and was held in high esteem by both my overseers and colleagues.

In the midst of my exciting and busy life, Hernando, a young doctor who had been my brother's friend since grammar school, swept me off my feet with his Latin charm. We went steady for two years and fell deeply in love. Mutti, who was aware of the Colombian men's tendency to be unfaithful, wasn't too keen on the idea of my marriage.

*   *   *   *   *   *

Vatti was the President of the Asociación de Austriacos Libres (Association of Free Austrians) in Colombia for two terms, and my parents were active in charitable and social activities. He was outspoken about his dream of becoming a grandfather. My first tragedy occurred when, Vatti, who had always been my best friend, died of a heart attack at the age of 52, shortly before our first baby, David, was born. I was inconsolable. I found the little cap he had treasured for his unborn grandson to wear to their first stadium soccer game together, and a little doll, in case my first baby would be a girl. This was the deepest grief I had experienced, and I still think of my dear Vatti every day.

*   *   *   *   *   *

Hernando, who had accomplished his Residency in Orthopedic Surgery at the National University Hospital in Bogotá, was honored with a scholarship for further training at the Hospital for Special Surgery in New York City.

I had to resign from my job at the Embassy and we left with our adorable and very active baby, David. I had been in New York before, enjoying all the fascinating sights and cultural outings. Now, being a young mother with a working husband, I saw New York from another angle. It was hectic but at the same time exciting. We befriended wonderful people and I spent many hours at Central Park, in the company of other young mothers and their babies.

Two years later we moved on to Pasadena, California, where Hernando won another two year Scholarship to major in Hand Surgery. Our second child, Alejandro, was born there. Our two adorable babies kept me very busy and were our pride and joy.

When Hernando finished his training we returned to live in Bogotá. After much sacrifice and hard work, Hernando´s career began to take off. I was often recommended by the American Embassy to translate texts for businesses and law firms, from home.

A year after we returned to Bogotá I gave birth to our youngest son, Ricardo, who added much happiness to our delightful family. The years we spent guiding our sons into young adulthood and forming them into good citizens, were the most fulfilling of my life.

Chapter 5

BUGANVILES

In 1974, Hernando and I bought a small, week-end farm that would provide a refuge from the hectic workdays in the capital. It was eleven acres square, located less than two hours from our home in Bogotá.

We named our get-away 'Buganviles' (a striking plant that blossoms in a variety of colors). The farm house was over a hundred years old and run-down, but part of the pleasure was remodeling it into a cozy, country home. The surrounding, natural beauty was heavenly.

There was a fountain that blended perfectly with the breathtaking, natural landscape and the pleasant tropical temperature, about 75 degrees Fahrenheit all-year-round, was a welcome change from the cool climate in Bogotá. To honor its name, we surrounded the fence with beautiful bougainvillea plants. The climate was warm enough to grow multicolored hibiscus, and cool enough for enormous hydrangeas that bloomed all year round.

We filled 'Buganviles' with many meaningful mementos, the most memorable was my antique hat collection. I unwrapped three generations of ladies' hats, seventy-three in all, which I had kept in boxes until we could display them on the walls of our family room. Some had been passed down to me by Omi and Mutti, and others were of my own choice. Some were extravagant, representing high fashion from the thirties, forties and fifties. They made an impressive collection and my friends and I enjoyed wearing them to costume parties. Another wall was decorated with a collection of match-boxes displaying logos of the hotels and restaurants we had visited. My parents started the collection in Vienna and many years later, Hernando and I added to it when we traveled to medical conventions overseas.

A rain forest bordered 'Buganviles' and a river, with stones along its banks, ran through its midst shaded by lovely, old trees with varieties of wild fern and parasites adorning their branches. It was an exotic and mysterious niche—pure delight for anyone who appreciates the beauty of nature.

One of our favorite family activities was fishing. Together with the children, we'd spend the morning by the banks of the river and then barbeque our catch in the garden. 'Buganviles' was a perfect place for entertaining and we usually had company. Our children would invite their friends and fill the house with laughter, games, giggles, and scraped knees.

An enchanting sense of freedom surrounded 'Buganviles'. I enjoyed 'chatting' with the birds, whistling to them while they hid in the colourful vegetation. Many years later, when my children had their own families, my little grand-daughters also enjoyed listening to how the birds answered my whistles when we established a friendly conversation. Some birds built their nests in the geranium baskets that hung from the columns, under the roof of our open terrace. It was delightful to watch them fly into the terrace and feed their babies, right above us. It wasn´t uncommon to enjoy a special moment watching a canary's first attempt at flying, a nest of baby bluebirds sharing an earthworm, or a woodpecker trying out different trees before deciding where to peck-out his home.

When we noticed an invasion of caterpillars in the garden, the air would soon be adorned with butterflies of amazing colors and designs. There was one extraordinary species that carried a perfect number 69 printed on its red wings. Someone believed this was a subliminal message and purchased a lottery ticket with this number. He never won.

It must have been the pleasure of being surrounded by such luscious vegetation that led me to develop a special interest in landscaping and I decided to study garden design. A whole new dimension filled my life as I found my niche in the world of plants and flowers.

Studying about gardens, I began to realize that the perfect combination of soil and climate at 'Buganviles' held unlimited potential for growing plants. I finished my studies at a college in Bogotá and partnered with Juan, an experienced gardener, to start a landscaping business. Many of the plants we needed for our gardening projects were rooted and nourished in our new, open air nursery and greenhouse.

There was a rose plantation of approximately fifteen hundred rose plants when we bought the property. They hadn't been well tended and required much work. I hired an Agronomist to teach me, and two workers to give them proper care. We grafted varieties of Meilland roses and got them to flourish beautifully. However, delivering cut roses to twelve flower shops at distant locations in Bogotá was a very time consuming and frustrating job. The constantly fluctuating demand made my business not only difficult, but sometimes unpleasant. Each client needed about three—hundred dozen roses on Mother's and Valentine's Days—which of course, I didn't have—and the rest of the year, they only wanted ten to twenty dozen per week. Often, I had to give the rest away.

I was discouraged by this situation and the fact that several enormous, rose export plantations were starting up in Colombia at the same time. This didn´t leave much space for a small business like mine. I'm not a good saleswoman, and didn't like selling perishable roses anyway, so I abandoned my rose business. In the end, it was a relief. The plants remained as a beautiful decoration piece that added to the pleasure of visiting 'Buganviles'.

A friend gave me a young 'guanábana' tree that flourished soon after it was transplanted. Guanábana is a big, tropical fruit with a creamy, sweet and slightly acid flavor. It has dark, green skin even when ripe and big black seeds imbedded in its tasty, white pulp. It is an exotic, tropical fruit that only grows in a few select places in the world. No one can refuse a delicious 'guanábana' juice or better yet, a 'guanabana' ice cream. There was enough land available at 'Buganviles' to start a new crop, and my 'guanábana' tree seemed a good fit. My agronomist advised me to grow this fruit on a commercial basis.

I purchased two hundred young 'guanábana' trees, about six feet tall, and planted them on the left side of the lake. When the trees had grown to their proper size, the agronomist, who was an expert in fruit, taught me and my workers the grafting technique called 'acodos aereos', a process that allows certain selected branches to produce their own, new roots. After two years of careful attention, when the branches had grown enough roots of their own, they were ready to be separated from the mother tree. Every grafted branch became an independent tree. In comparison to starting out from seedlings, this technique saves the farmers about six years in their growing process. We worked hard and grafted eight hundred young 'guanábana' trees.

Our landscaping business was becoming successful. Not only were we called on to decorate the gardens of luxury homes and apartment complexes in Bogotá, but several gardens in other cities. One of our main contracts was to landscape a new shopping mall that was being built in the city of Ipiales, at the border between Colombia and Ecuador. The only garden supplies available in the area were the earth and fertilizers, which meant the trees, plants and everything else had to be transported from Bogotá in a twelve-wheel truck.

In 1978 a prestigious construction firm assigned us the landscaping of a luxurious apartment complex and over the next fourteen years, we signed many contracts with them. Unfortunately, violence among the drug traffickers caused a long period of recession, driving most construction firms into bankruptcy. We worked for another company for three years, until landscaping became a luxury that their clients couldn't afford. No one ever called us again, not even for an estimate.

I was glad to have Buganviles' and hoped someday to retire there. My dream was to spend my last years surrounded by its natural beauty—such an integral part of my happiness. I could never be inactive there. The chores were endless, and being so close to Bogotá I could live at home with my family and spend two days a week working at the farm. Often, we hosted our friends on short vacations—'Buganviles' was a perfect sanctuary for anyone who needed a getaway.

Jaider and Gladys, our farm caretakers and their three children were like family to me. They earned more than anybody else in the area and were treated with respect and affection. Their privileged condition was evident by the number of friends and relatives who asked them to be 'padrinos' (God parents) to their children. I had every reason to believe they felt the same affection toward us.

Some of the neighbors were my long-standing friends and I made a point of contributing to neighborhood activities. We watched our boys, and the youngsters that played with them in their early years, grow into adulthood and go their own ways.

My family life was not without sadness. After fourteen years, my happy marriage to Hernando began to fall apart. Although I tried desperately to save it, we divorced in 1977. The boys stayed with me and saw their father often. This was a very difficult time in my life but I learned to live without him and fend for myself. My sons gave me the inspiration to fight on.

David studied Business Administration and his first job was at a bank. Five years later he decided to work independently and started his own import-export enterprise.

In 1987, Alejandro graduated from Medical School. After finishing his year of rural training, he left for the United States to do his Residency in Psychiatry. Although I missed him very much, it was comforting to know that things were going well for him. He married an American girl, the daughter of his professor, and started a lovely family.

My youngest son, Ricardo, also studied Medicine and became an Orthopedic Surgeon, like his father. They all married at early ages. My four grand-daughters and two grandsons became God´s most marvelous gifts to me.

In the early nineties, David and Ricardo moved away from Bogotá with their families. This was a new stage in my life and I wanted to be free to visit them on holidays or whenever I was needed.

During the economic recession, the Colombian peso fell from 1.000 to 3.000 pesos per dollar in just one year. The frequent kidnappings by the FARC, ELN and Paramilitaries, and the brutal violence of the drug traffickers prevented people from traveling or buying any rural property in Colombia.

My sons were concerned for my safety and insisted that I try to sell 'Buganviles' as soon as possible. After much deliberating, I took their advice and visited a realtor in Anapoima, the neighboring town. It was a difficult decision. I had spent the last twenty-six years working on my little 'paradise' and would probably have to exchange it for a property of much less value in Bogotá. And, how I would miss the gorgeous greenery, the birds, my dogs, and those delightful family breakfasts on the terrace! So much of my life had revolved around the pleasure of working this land and it had been of invaluable comfort when healing the sadness of my divorce. However, this was no time to look back, my security was in danger and life had to go on.

The realtor finally found a family that wanted to exchange 'Buganviles' for a small condo in Bogotá. They were two brothers, who were probably smart enough to appreciate the future potential of one thousand 'guanábana' trees growing on the property. 'Buganviles' was located between the two cities where they lived so they could have their mother at a comfortable distance from both of their homes. Every member of their family had visited 'Buganviles' and Ricardo and I had seen their condo in Bogotá. It was small and not very well located, but we knew that many people in Colombia lost everything when they had to abandon their farms. I considered myself lucky to have this only option. The realtor informed me that his clients wanted to close the deal, so we invited them for a barbecue the following Saturday. It was that awful Tuesday morning, when I went to put things in order for their visit that the bandits came to kidnap me.

Chapter 6

THE CAMPAMENTO (CAMP)

Slowly, we drew near to a group of small tents and a tin shack. It was getting dark and I couldn't see much, but I noticed a group of 'guerrilleros', idly standing around.

Some people approached me, whom I immediately identified as captives. Their bowed heads told the tale of forced submission and suffering. It was heart-breaking to see them, especially because it gave me a glimpse of what I was in for. And yet it was comforting to know I wouldn't be alone among the odious FARC characters. From the terrorist attacks shown in the news, and interviews of kidnapped victims, I had seen how poisoned their minds were against their hostages. The boys leading my horse might have been respectful, decent youth if they hadn't been indoctrinated otherwise.

Two of the captives helped me off the horse, I was so sore that I could barely stand on my feet. It was truly nothing less than a miracle that I hadn't fractured any bones.

The 'comandante' came forward and told Blanca, the only female hostage, "Take her ta yar tent, she'll stay with ya".

Blanca´s hair was untidy and her expression was at first, without life. Soon, I found that she was a warm, compassionate woman; there was immediate empathy between us. My heart went out to her sad eyes and I could feel her sympathy in return. Although she tried hard not to show it, she silently communicated her distress.

"Come, dear and meet our companions", she said putting her arm around my shoulder.

There were six men in the group. Two were in their sixties, one was close to eighty, and the other three were much younger. When one young man greeted me by flashlight, I caught a glimpse of tears in his eyes. I must have been a pitiful sight after all I had been through those past days. The next day he told me that I reminded him of his mother.

Blanca went to fetch a small pot with rice and lentils. One of the young men went to warm up some water while I devoured the unsavory food. She handed me a sweat-suit and three woolen socks. Someone gave me two aspirins and cup of 'aguapanela' (brown sugar tea) which I appreciated immensely. Aside from the cold and the shivering, I had a splitting headache.

Everyone wanted to help me in some way by sharing the little they had. One of the young men lent me a sweater and another gave me five, unmatched woolen socks. Each one relinquished his offering with reverence, as if it was the most precious treasure. I soon learned how valuable those small items were under the circumstances. Blanca gave me two tee-shirts and two men's underpants that her husband had left behind when he was released. I tried not to imagine how many people had used them before.

My clothes, hair, face and hands were encrusted with mud, and my skin was dry and burned from the wind. Blanca told me, "You'll feel better after you take a bath."

Soon, two of the young men returned carrying a big pot with warm water and a small empty pot to pour water over my back. They moved away so that I could remove my clothes. The warm water felt good but it only stayed warm for about two minutes. I was aching all over and there was no strength left in me.

The only available light came from a small fire built on the dirt floor of the shack where they cooked the meals. Mental images of darkness, cold and desolation hit me full force. As soon as I could walk, a 'guerrillero' escorted Blanca and me to the tent with his flashlight.

She whispered under her breath, "Oh, boy, you're getting the royal treatment tonight. Don´t expect it to be like that from tomorrow on. If the weather is OK, we'll wash your clothes in the morning."

The 'bed' was made of four logs placed in the shape of a rectangle on the muddy ground, and filled with dried grass turned into straw. Blanca laid a small piece of cloth on the straw—a pillow was out of question.

"Before we lie down we have to inspect the straw for black, hairy worms. They bite and cause a painful burn that can make you very, very sick". We talked for a long while.

"They captured us ten weeks ago when my 'papito' (Daddy, meaning her husband) and I were arriving at our farm in 'Cachipay'. You can't imagine what we've been through. Two weeks later they sent him away to get three million U.S. dollars for our ransom. I'll have to stay here forever—he'll only be able to round up a very small fraction of such an outrageous amount."

Blanca told me she had two married sons, a daughter, and five grandchildren. Her daughter was due to have her first baby next month.

"You can imagine how I feel about not being there to help her," she wept.

The relentless cold combined with my worries and sorrow made it impossible for me to relax. Blanca wanted to share her blanket but it was too small to cover both of us. Every couple of hours, the 'guerrillero' on duty shone a flashlight in our faces.

"Just checkin' if ya're dead or not".

On this first, sleepless, rainy night, I had to leave the tent to urinate five times. I was terrified that a snake could crawl into the tent, but I tried not to lose my composure so poor Blanca could get some sleep.

"Don't worry about snakes, dear—only non-poisonous ones can live in this cold climate," Blanca said. But just the thought of any snake creeping into my bed was more than I could bear.

"The only animals we see around here are the hawks flying above us, waiting for their prey—just like our captors."

The temperature was normally around thirty five degrees Fahrenheit and according to Blanca, the altitude was approximately 13.000 feet (as high as the top of Pike's Peak in the U.S.). Blanca and I comforted each other when sadness invaded our thoughts and we needed to talk or cry. I had difficulty catching my breath. Depression set in and I couldn't get warm enough to stop shivering. The things we had spoken of came and went in my mind until I finally fell asleep for a little while.

It was still dark when we woke up to the "guerrilleros" cursing and screaming at the top of their lungs in their vulgar language.

"They wake us up every day when they start the fire for breakfast. They call themselves a 'military force', which makes them think they have to get up early, even if they spend the rest of the day just loafing around," Blanca said.

Our tent was no more than a piece of camouflaged army canvas lifted off the muddy ground by a central pole and eight wooden sticks, pitched on the edge of a cliff like a beach tent. There was nothing to stop the wind from blowing right through the lower part of the tent. A sheet of black plastic covered the opening where we crawled in and out. Condensed water dripped off the camouflaged canvas roof, leaving a puddle of mud around our 'bed'. Blanca's blanket was always damp. She kept her few belongings in a little plastic bag which she also used to cover her feet.

The next morning I was given a small, dented aluminum pot and a spoon. They served soup for breakfast (if you can call salted water with rice and a few noodles, soup). I was introduced to their 'cancharinas', a mixture of flour, water and salt. They mashed the dough with their dirty hands, and fried it in lard. They didn't taste any better than they looked.

After we washed our pots, they gave us a drink made of hot water and chocolate. Everything tasted awful and the sanitary conditions were revolting. I went back to the tent, lay on the scratchy straw and stared at the camouflaged cloth above me. I wanted to cry but there were no tears left. I wanted to scream but I couldn´t utter a sound. I wanted to die but I knew that my family was waiting for me to return alive.

When I asked Blanca what they used for a bathroom she said she would take me there, "It's called the 'chonto' and is only a long, narrow ditch where we go when we need to have a bowel movement. We use the mud piled on the side of the trench to cover it up when we're done. I know it's very annoying, but you'll get used to having a 'guerrillero' pointing a gun at you while you're there."

I became constipated for four days after I saw the 'chonto'. This wasn't the first time I had been to the bathroom in the woods. Often, my family and I would go on camping trips with our friends and their children. But that was different. We always took a little toilet seat and placed three wooden sticks with a long plastic sheet around them for 'walls' and a plastic 'door', that we set up in a discrete place to protect everyone´s privacy. The worst thing about the FARC 'chonto' was not only the lack of privacy, but feeling that one has been robbed of any human dignity. This normal, everyday activity became something dreaded and distressful.

Aside from a few stubble bushes, the only vegetation in the area was a plant with long, white, velvety leaves called 'frailejón'. Blanca told me sometimes we would have to use these leaves as a substitute for toilet paper, and young women even had to use them for sanitary napkins, a luxury not always available. 'Frailejón' plants only grow at very high altitudes, above the tree-line. No wonder I was having difficulty breathing.

When it stopped raining, Blanca came to the tent, "Come out, Myriam, our companions want to know everything about you". She was trying hard to cheer me up.

My fellow companions were standing on the only green spot in sight. From a distance, it looked like very green grass but when I arrived, I saw that it was like everything else around us—nothing more than soggy, green moss covering the heavy mud, making it impossible to sit on. The only way we could converse was to stand in the deep mud. There wasn't even a log close by and the few rocks in sight were too far apart and too large and heavy to be moved.

The male hostages were even more uncomfortable than Blanca and I. Their sleeping accommodations were in the shack where the 'guerrilleros' cooked the food. It had a dirt floor, and a rusty, tin roof. On one side was a 'bed' for three people, similar to ours. The remaining space in the first 'room' was an open passageway they called the 'club' where our captors hung around most of the time. They would sit on the 'bed' even when the hostages were trying to get some sleep. The wind never stopped blowing through the shack.

The cooking place they called the 'rancha', was in the middle of the open passageway. Three iron poles supported a horizontal iron stick where they hung two cooking pots over a fire. A few sacks with rice were the only 'benches' available if you wanted to sit down in the 'club'.

Another 'room' had been added to the men´s quarters to accomodate three more kidnapped men. They propped up about eight square feet of rusty tin against the existing 'wall' and two wooden poles were added to cover another makeshift 'bed'. It was slightly better than sleeping outside in the freezing, open air. The 'guerrilleros' made noise and carried on all the time. Their utter disrespect for their victims' need for rest and privacy was inhuman.

This small shack, where the six male hostages slept, was also the common gathering place. There was nowhere else to stand when it was raining—and it rained almost all the time. Nobody in the civilized world could imagine the conditions we were forced to endure. When I was finally able to face reality, I regretted not having a camera.

There was no fence around the 'Camp' but it was quite unnecessary. Who would think to go anywhere with seven armed 'guerrilleros' on guard, ready to follow orders and shoot anyone who made the smallest attempt at escape?

Chapter 7

MY FELLOW HOSTAGES

MANUEL WAS A 28-year-old rancher, and also a pilot. He and his wife were captured when travelling with their two very young children to visit her parents.

Manuel was crying when he told me, "The thugs placed a large log across the road, pulled Julia and me out of the van at gunpoint and pushed us into a waiting truck. Our babies were in panic, screaming there on the road. Thank God their nanny was with us. She loves them and has been with us since our little girl was born. I trust she stopped a car and asked them to take her to Julia's parents in Villavicencio. Three weeks later the FARC sent Julia back to collect three thousand million pesos (one million U.S.) to pay for our freedom. I haven't heard from her since. Even if my brothers could sell my parents' farm, we wouldn´t have that kind of money."

I cried. He was a tall, slender, good-looking young man with hazel eyes, long brown hair, and a thin beard. Blanca had already told me how kind he was—always ready to help the others. He came from a wealthy family in one of Bogotá's neighboring provinces. By the time I arrived, he had already been captive for thirteen months in nine different locations.

"I've been caught in the middle of armed attacks between the FARC and the Army twice, while we were running from one camp to another. You never know where to run when they start dropping rockets from the helicopters."

Victor, a thirty-three year old doctor, was also dragged out of his van while returning from a short trip. He lived in a small city in the Llanos Orientales (Eastern Plains). He and his wife, who was also a doctor, had three small children. Victor was not tall; he had black, curly hair and a kind face. According to Blanca, he was a considerate, warm-hearted doctor.

Victor told me, "Thirteen neighbors in our housing complex of eighty apartments have been kidnapped over the last six years." When I asked him how they could remain there at such high risk, he answered, "You know how hard it is for doctors to start over in another city. Most of my patients live in the same area. And tell me—where is anyone safe nowadays?"

Federico, a forty year old engineer, was abducted on the road while he was writing up an estimate for a new contract. Federico and Victor were living their tragic adventure together. They were abducted on the same day and taken away in the same taxi. It wasn't strange that they had become close friends and supported each other throughout the ordeal. Federico was losing his hair, which made his sunburn more prominent. You could see from the way his clothes fit that he had lost a lot of weight. He was confident that his wife, Gloria, who was a lawyer, was doing a good job with his negotiation. They had a fourteen year old daughter and a twelve year old boy.

Federico's strong, positive and easy-going personality helped him cope with the depressing circumstances and adapt to this situation better than anyone else. I enjoyed talking with him—his uncompromising optimism was contagious and we were soon good friends.

Carlos, age 69, was the owner of a duffle-bag stand at the marketplace in a town near Buganviles. His business was barely profitable enough to feed himself, his daughter and his grandchild. It was obvious that he had been kidnapped by mistake.

"Nobody in my family has any money, and if they did, I doubt they'd spend it on my ransom," he told me, sadly. Carlos was short and stout with grayish hair. He had been captured only a week before me so he hadn't lost much weight yet.

Benjamín, 78, owned a cattle farm. "They captured me at my home while I was having lunch with my wife and daughter. Eight bandits invaded our terrace, shooting into the air. My poor wife fainted when they dragged me away," he said. Blanca told me he always had a kind word for everyone, even for the 'guerrilleros'. She was worried about Benjamín because he wasn't getting his medication.

Pedro was a 60 year old a potato farmer. He had once owned several buildings in Bogotá but like many Colombians at this time, he lost everything and was now bankrupt. He was a short, grey haired, thin man. It wasn't hard to see that he had a conflictive personality and soon I found out that he didn't get along with Manuel, his tent mate. His face reflected bitterness. Back in our tent, Blanca told me about the day she and her 'papito' arrived at the camp.

When her husband heard Pedro's name, he approached him and said, "This is certainly a small world! You meet people in the strangest places! I've been trying to locate you for over a year. I left you dozens of messages at your office in Bogotá, asking you to please pay for the repairs we did on your building. I always heard your voice in the background saying, "Tell him I'm away on a trip!" The next day they became friends.

Even though Blanca, Pedro, Carlos and I had been kidnapped in the same area, within ten miles of Buganviles, we'd never met before. Federico, Victor and Manuel were captured while driving on the highway to the Eastern Plains.

The FARC kidnapping 'technique' people on the roads is called 'Pesca Milagrosa' (Miracle Fishing). When someone is caught this way, the FARC bandits don't know whom they are catching and select their prey according to the type of car they drive. They set up a roadblock after a curve that can't be seen by the victim as he approaches. Once someone falls into their trap, there is no going back and they extort everything they can from the family.

I was very concerned about my son, David, who often traveled with his family to their country house three hours away from Bogotá.

My thoughtful group of kidnapped friends gathered for prayer every evening at around six o'clock. We stood in a circle, held hands, and begged God for His mercy. The faith we had that He would answer and our mutual support, helped to relieve some of the unrelenting tension. It was Victor's turn to lead the prayer on my first evening at the camp. He thanked God for the food and for my safe arrival. Then we prayed for our families and our captors, asking our Lord's help for the FARC and our families to come to fair agreements whenever He saw fit for any one of us to be released. I thought to myself, "How much is a 'fair agreement' in the eyes of these cruel beasts? What could possibly seem fair to them?"

It was incomprehensible to me that such terrorist actions could go unpunished in our country. We were taught in Elementary School that the first law in the Constitution is to protect the lives, honor and property of its citizens. What was the Pastrana government doing to stop these crimes? Now that I was a victim, I began to consider new angles of the situation. Some of the non-governmental organizations (NGOs) operating in Colombia, were partial to the FARC and made their opinions known around the world. They must have been aware of what was going on—were they even reporting the kidnappings to organizations in their countries? Were they taking any serious action? They seemed to be only concerned about 'human rights' that translated into 'guerrilla's rights'. What about our rights?

Chapter 8

THE THIRD DAY

SIMÓN, THE 'COMANDANTE' in charge of our group, was about 23 years old. He was a short, thin man with three of his front teeth missing. Two days after my arrival he came to my tent carrying a notebook and pen and told me the 'FARC High Authorities' needed information about my financial status.

My companions, Federico and Manuel, had already given me a crash course in preparation for this first interview. They advised me to tell the truth, stick to the questions, and never volunteer extra information.

"Always keep in mind, with no exceptions, that we are only a sum of money to these guys. You and I know that no one's going free if the family doesn't pay. They've done their homework, they know exactly what you own," they said.

Simon's interview began, "I hear ya're a damn rich woman—so, what' we have?"

"My sons and I own a house in Bogotá and a small farm near Anapoima". He asked where I lived and I saw how illiterate he was when he took such a painfully long time to scribble down the address that had to be corrected after he was done. He probably never finished second grade.

"I need the numbas of two guys in yar fam'ly". I had no choice but to give him David's and my brother, Martin's, phone numbers. I had been told they usually demand an outrageous figure at first, something impossible for any prosperous, working family to attain. Sometimes, if the victim is very lucky, they will negotiate the sum and free him or her after signing an IOU. If the family doesn't pay on the agreed date, someone in the family will be killed or kidnapped again. In order to avoid empowering the Guerillas, there is a law in Colombia that prohibits families from paying ransoms, even though the life of their loved one is at stake. Therefore, if the victim is released after the family pays the agreed amount, this transaction must not be revealed to the authorities.

Chapter 9

WASHING AND BATHING

When the rain finally stopped for a while, Blanca told me we should bathe and do our laundry. The warm water on the evening of my arrival was evidently a privilege that wouldn't be repeated. After we asked for permission, Blanca and I made our way through an enormous swamp, to the assigned bathing spot.

After we undressed, leaving on our longest T-shirt, we approached the brook and climbed down the muddy steps into the freezing water. One of our captors was always nearby, pointing his gun at us.

Blanca knew how miserable I felt and told me, "Just ignore him Myriam, you'll get used to this."

I washed as fast as I could but not without catching a terrible headache from the freezing water. All I wanted was to get out of there as fast as possible. Blanca had a tiny towel which she passed on to me when she finished drying her body. We poured some icy water on our feet and put our dirty socks on again. The bathing process added new trauma to the already desperate state I was in. Once again, something so basic and necessary became a huge issue.

We walked a bit further along the brook and reached the 'laundry area', where there were two slightly level stones with a large, flat stone placed horizontally on top. Blanca picked some 'frailejón' leaves and put them on the ground to protect our knees from the rough rock we had to kneel on while we scrubbed our underwear.

A few years earlier, a Rheumatologist warned me that if I wanted to keep my swollen joints from hurting, I should always throw everything in the washer and never put my hands in cold water. The subject had been forgotten to me but as my hands grew sore, I remembered the doctor's words. My clothes weren´t very clean when we were done but the most difficult part was how to dry them in the constant drizzle. We waited for every moment of sunshine to hang out our 'laundry', and rushed to put it away in a plastic bag inside our tent when the rain started up again.

While we were standing around talking that afternoon, I suddenly felt dizzy and became very weak. Luckily, my companions noticed something was wrong and caught me just before I collapsed. They carried me to my tent and gave me something to drink. Victor, our doctor, was very concerned and told the 'comandante' that I needed my medicine immediately because of my high blood pressure, and the high altitude could be fatal. As usual the answer was,

"She'll havit ba' tamorro." I fainted again a week later but never received any medicine.

Each of us wrote our family a note to have ready when the first lucky person to be released could take it back. Manuel, the young pilot, managed to get two sheets of paper that he divided into small pieces. Victor had a pen. We wrote the notes and hid them, waiting for that golden opportunity to send them home. I hid mine in my sock. Manuel made lists of our home phone numbers and gave each of us a copy.

My friendship with Blanca grew as time went on. We talked about our past, our families, and soon we felt as if we had been friends our whole lives. She told me about her husband, 'Papito' and his 'romantic adventures.' The more I listened to her, the more relieved I was that I didn't have to put up with my own 'Papito' any more.

Our conversations helped us maintain our faith in God and hold on to the belief that we still had a future to fight for. We shared recipes and agreed to try them as soon as we returned home. Blanca had a small collection of possessions she had acquired one by one during her time in captivity.

"I 'took' the 'pillowcase' we are using from a camp where we stayed," she said. The 'pillowcase' was made of many small pieces of material roughly sewn together by hand. It was coming apart. Of course it couldn´t compare to a pillow, but it was better than laying our heads directly on the dry, scratchy straw where black, hairy worms crawled. I told Blanca that I had 'acquired' my little blanket the first morning after I was kidnapped, much the same way.

"You learn fast, Myriam, I'm proud of you," she said.

Chapter 10

OUR MENU

ONE MORNING WE saw a herd of mules waddling down another mountain nearby, loaded with big sacks hanging off their sides. Blanca told me they came every week, carrying 'la remesa' (the food supplies) to the main camp where they would be distributed to nine similar camps in the area. Watching those mules was the most exciting event of the week and I hopefully imagined that perhaps something different would appear on our menu—but no such luck. Every breakfast, lunch and dinner were made from variations of the following list:

Rice and lentils

Cancharinas (fried flour tarts)

Sapitos, (the same flour tarts, with sugar on top)

Arepas, round, flat corn tarts

Or, once a month, something especially delicious; a blend of lentils with a sardine . . . Wow!

Aguapanela (the brown sugar tea I mentioned earlier)

Chocolate cooked in water

Sometimes, when our captors were feeling particularly generous, they gave us 'aguapanela' (brown-sugar tea) mixed with crushed saltine crackers. When I asked if I could have my saltines separately, I was told that by the time they reached the camp, they were always in crumbs.

Victor advised me to make a special effort to eat more, "You need to be healthy in order to survive what's coming and starvation isn't going to help your state of mind. They'll move us to different camps when you least expect it and those journeys by foot are long and strenuous."

I had no appetite but I forced myself to eat small amounts of the disgusting food. My usual diet included mostly healthy foods—Oh those delicious tropical fruits and fresh vegetables! At home, I always tried to have sufficient protein, and sometimes indulged in a dessert or ice cream. We certainly wouldn't get any of that!

Chapter 11

ESCAPE?

WE WERE ALL talking while standing in the mud one morning when Carlos asked, "What are our chances of escaping? Do you think we can get our hands on some food and a map, and even a weapon and a horse?"

"Are you kidding Carlos? A horse can't live around here. As far as I know, horses don't eat rice and lentils and there isn't any grass in this wilderness. Wake up, hermano (brother)—you're too optimistic!" Federico answered. "Only two or three out of the hundreds who try to escape are successful, and most likely they have help from insiders. There's no way we could reach civilization on our own. There aren't even leaves to eat while crossing the 'páramo' (freezing moor)."

"Besides, there are eight more camps like this one in the area. When someone is missing, they send out 'guerrilleros' from every camp to track down whoever escapes. They take them back to the camp and shoot them," Manuel added.

"When we first came, Victor, Manuel and I tried to hide a few cans of tuna fish and crackers. We were searching for a pistol and working on escape plans. Just a few days later they brought in a young couple, Marlen and Efraín. From the jewellery they were wearing, we figured he was probably a 'Mafioso' (a drug lord). They were travelling in their Mercedes to Villavicencio for their honeymoon when they were kidnapped. Since money was no problem for him, Efraín promised a 'guerrillero' that he would be rewarded with a farm and a truck if he would help them escape and guide them to safety."

"One night, the three of them escaped. They weren´t missed until the next morning at breakfast. By that time, they were quite far from the camp but still on the mountain-range, in FARC territory. They didn't get very far. Bandits from other camps were sent out in all directions to find them and had them dragged back to the Compañía before noon."

"What happened to them?" I asked.

"They held a pantomime Court Martial and then shot Marlen and the 'guerrillero' in the presence of Efraín. It was horrendous—that poor guy was crazy about her!"

"About a week later, William, one of the guerrilleros in our camp, went to the Compañia. When he returned, he told us he had seen Efrain tied to a tree with a heavy chain. He was going to be kept there until his family paid the ransom," Federico continued.

"Did they finally send him home?" I asked.

"Yes, they shot him and sent his body home to his family in a black plastic bag. That's what the FARC do when someone tries to escape." Needless to say, our friends changed their minds.

Chapter 12

OUTFITTED BY THE FARC

On my fifth day in captivity, my stomach was stopped-up and aching so badly, I asked Victor if there was any medicine available in the camp. He suggested two tablespoons of cooking oil. I found an empty bottle in the mud, washed it, and asked William, the least hostile of the 'guerilleros', to please get me some oil for medicine. He complied. By this time, the skin on my face was unusually dry and my lips were cracked and painful. These conditions are common to high altitudes. Our captors used chap-stick but there was no chance of getting any for us. From then on, Blanca and I used cooking oil on our faces every night. I asked Victor if we could use the oil as a day cream but he said it could cause serious sunburn.

I remembered reading in the paper that the FARC had signed a commitment to stop kidnapping people over sixty or children under twelve. I was sixty two, but I let on that I was sixty-eight. Of course this made no difference. The FARC don't respect their agreements anyway.

I asked Simón to please order a hat for me, hoping that my age, my physical weaknesses or an illness might motivate them to set me free or at least treat me with some decency and respect. Of course this was only wishful thinking.

Nobody's medicine ever arrived. I learned quickly that all we could depend on when we were in need was the kindness of our companions.

Manuel and Federico advised me to be brave and not act older than I really was. They said it wouldn't help me at all, on the contrary, thinking this way would only increase my depression. I took their advice and they were glad to see my overall condition improve after the first week.

I finally received my FARC supplies: a camouflaged guerrilla uniform, a pair of old, smelly, rubber boots with a hole in each sole, a light weight sweat suit, a bra the size of a ten-year old, and two men's underpants. There was also a bar of laundry soap and a roll of toilet paper—and no shampoo. When I asked Simón for a comb, a mirror and toothpaste, he told me the FARC didn't have any combs or mirrors for their 'guests', but he did give me a small tube of Colgate toothpaste. The filthy toothbrush assigned to me must have been in use for at least a year! Its bristles were in disarray and caked with grime. I was speechless!

Federico was standing nearby and saw my tears as I clasped the sickening thing in my hand. He also noticed how embarrassed I was to wipe my tears and my nose on my sleeve. Without a word, he pulled an old kitchen towel out of his pocket, tore it in half, and gently handed me a piece. I'll never forget Federico's kind gesture.

Victor put his arm around my shoulder and said,

"Myriam, be patient. Protesting won't help. Some of us aren't lucky enough to get a new toothbrush. I've learned to get by with very few belongings over these past six months of captivity. Little by little, you will too."

Whether I liked it or not, this was going to be my tooth-brush for the time being, so I dropped the repulsive thing in boiling water and tried to get it off my mind—until the next morning.

I wore everything I owned, day and night. Now that I had a 'new wardrobe', at least I could wash what had been next to my body, from time to time. As soon as Simón delivered my 'endowment', I returned the sweater, blanket, and other things my companions had so kindly lent me on the night of my arrival. I knew how much they needed them.

Soon, I became attached to my fellow hostages and felt very fortunate to have their companionship. There was warmth and a sense of caring among us, especially when someone was depressed—which happened all the time. Crying was a natural reaction and at least one of us needed encouragement every day. I knew that some other kidnapped people, especially the most wealthy, were completely isolated and often tortured for information. Being alone with these wild, FARC characters, without a gentle and sensible person to speak with, would have been too horrifying to consider.

When he saw the swollen joints on my hands, Carlos went to his tent and returned with a pair of black, woolen gloves.

"Myriam needs them more than anyone else," he said.

I was thrilled by his thoughtfulness and once I managed to get my circulation going, by rubbing my hands on the back of my neck, the gloves kept them warm. Both the gelid wind and the occasional, burning sun were harsh on my skin and eyes. Federico made me a walking stick and sometimes, Pedro, our gruff potato farmer, lent me his hat.

Two days earlier I found a blue jacket with orange lining in the mud. I didn't have anything else to protect me from the cold so I pulled it out of the mud, scrubbed it thoroughly, and hung it out to dry. It was a torn mess and had no zipper but I was in no position to be choosy. The dilapidated jacket matched the rest of my 'highly fashionable' wardrobe perfectly, and it was warmer than anything else available. I had no access to a piece of thread and a needle, but Blanca told me to wait, "Maybe if we catch Sandra (one of the 'guerilleras') in a good mood, we can ask her to lend us her needle." As soon as my jacket was dry enough, I wore it just as it was.

Chapter 13

NEGOTIATION

Meanwhile in Bogotá:

When I was released, David explained to me how the people who worked behind the scenes to obtain my freedom proceeded, and managed to come to a final agreement with the FARC.

It all started in Bogotá, the day after my kidnapping, and continued simultaneously throughout the time of my captivity, those long months. Of course each case is different; however, I hope that some of this information will be useful to other distressed families under similar circumstances.

When David arrived in Bogotá, my sons chose the people they wanted on the 'Comité' (Committee). It was a sensitive request to ask someone to make this sacrifice; negotiations can be time-consuming, frustrating, and risky. Each one of these friends had to commit to being available over an indefinite length of time. Nobody knew how long the process would last or how it would end. The general advice they followed, was not to have more than one close relative on the Comité because of the emotional pressure the bandits use to get their way. Everyone they asked to join accepted.

MEMBERS OF THE COMITÉ:

Captain Perez was chosen to be the Chairman. His invaluable experience resolving other negotiations inspired confidence in his ability to lead the team. It was also important to have a woman on the Comité, who could see things from a feminine viewpoint and anticipate my reactions.

My sons approached a lady who had held an important position in a past government. She is the aunt of my daughter-in-law and had cooperated in a similar Comité during the abduction of a close friend.

The other members were David, my ex-husband Hernando, and David's two best friends; the Dean of Economics at a University and the Manager of one of Colombia's largest flower plantations. I couldn't have asked for a better team. Even though most of them didn't know me personally, they concentrated their efforts, intelligence, and emotions on one goal during those long months: to save my life. God bless each one of them.

The operating guidelines for the Comité were as follows:

* Absolute secrecy regarding the meetings and themes discussed.
* Other members of my family who were not on the Comité could have a voice in the procedures but were not allowed to vote.
* Each member had to be present at every meeting.
* Every action was to be approved by the Chairman.
* The chosen spokesman or negotiator was the only individual permitted to maintain phone contact with the FARC representative. If necessary, they would pick a temporary replacement.
* The 'Comité' would meet every evening at six p.m.
* On Saturdays, they would meet at 10:30 a.m.

* Meetings would sometimes be held on Sundays. Everybody agreed to be available at a moment´s notice in case of an emergency.

* The negotiator should never improvise when discussing a matter with the FARC negotiator. Everything had to be previously approved by the Comité. If his opponent surprised him with something new, or tried to pressure him on the spot, he should cut off the conversation, immediately.

* The FARC's demands would never be accepted right away. Every time they made contact, our spokesman was to ask for time to study their proposal. This permitted the Comité to write up a coherent, counter-proposal to present on their next call.

* The objective was to maintain a verbal tug-of—war, forcing the FARC to bring the ransom down. The strategy consisted in trying to 'carefully climb up the stairs while bringing the FARC's demand down on the elevator'.

Hernando, my ex-husband, was assigned to visit the hostages that had been in captivity with me on their release when they called to deliver my notes. My son, Ricardo, who worked in another city, traveled to Bogotá every weekend to attend the Comité, and help in whatever way he could be useful.

Kidnappings are rampant in Colombia and most decent people feel not only honored, but duty bound to accept the request to be part of such a Comité. Groups of Colombians have established a Union of Cooperation that works hand-in-hand to rescue the kidnapped and help their families. The time they offer is a voluntary, token of solidarity, and they never accept compensation.

Chapter 14

RAFAEL

THREE GLOOMY WEEKS had passed and as always, we were watching the gray, barren, Andes mountain range, hoping to see something that might break the monotony of our daily existence. Suddenly, we saw three people descending one of the mountains—one was riding a horse.

"It looks like they are bringing another hostage!" Victor said.

"More millions are coming in! We'll be sooooo #%$&/?(%# "rich!" Our captors jumped and shouted, expressing their delight with the usual, filthy language.

| It took the newcomers a long time to arrive. I couldn't help but shed a tear when I saw the poor man on the horse. It was difficult to say how old he was because of the effects of the journey, and he seemed to be very, very sick. His name was Rafael.

Each of us gave the newcomer something to wear. Blanca was especially generous since her husband had left behind several, warm things. I remembered how kind my friends had been when I arrived under similar conditions and took off my 'new' blue jacket with the orange lining and lent it to Rafael until he received his own FARC 'endowment'.

He had been captured on his way home four nights earlier, and dragged through the same miserable adventure as the rest of us. The next day, he told us he was a lawyer from Cachipay, a town not far from Buganviles. He also told us he had epilepsy, and was particularly concerned because he needed to take very strong medicine every day of his life. He feared he would convulse at any time. Simón called his superior on the radio to report Rafael's condition and then assured Victor that the medicine would be sent to the camp the next day. Needless to say, the medicine never arrived.

You could tell Rafael had been rather handsome in his youth. He was medium height, with thick, black hair, and well-proportioned features.

This is how he described his past, "When I was a teenager, I was trained in a Seminary to become a Catholic priest but I had to leave the priesthood because I couldn't resist the temptation of women. I married Carmencita, a school teacher, who lived up to the important qualities expected of a bride, primarily, her virginity. Nine months after the wedding we had a son. Shortly after marrying Carmencita I had an affair with her sister, Consuelo. She gave birth to a daughter."

He ended up leaving both sisters and their children to live with a much younger girl in a small town. He kept a friendly relationship with his ex-wife but abandoned Consuelo and their little daughter. By the time she was sixteen, the girl was an alcoholic and had a child of her own. She finally located Rafael but he did nothing to help her.

"I'm better off getting out of town for a while because a fifteen year peasant girl is suing me on a paternity charge," he said.

Although he admitted he was the father, his position was, "I'm not going to accept responsibility for that child because I could be the mother's grandfather and 'she tricked me into it'."

He was clearly very proud of his 'super-macho' powers, and had no problem volunteering all this information without shame. Most of us were appalled by our new companion's behavior. In my opinion, Rafael was a narcissist who wanted everyone to be aware of his irresistible power over women, and from his long list of irresponsible relationships, he was also a freeloader. This was confirmed when I saw our companion, Victor the doctor, wearing my dilapidated blue jacket.

Victor had recently cured Simón of an eye infection. Surprisingly, in gratitude, Simón gave him a new, quilted, green jacket. Next thing we knew, Rafael was wearing Victor's new, green jacket, while Victor was wearing my worn out blue jacket with the orange lining.

When I asked Victor why he wasn't wearing his new jacket, he answered, "I accepted Rafael´s request to exchange jackets. He felt insulted to wear such a shabby thing, and I felt sorry for him. It makes no difference to me."

I knew this was the end of my only warm jacket and regretted having been naive enough to lend it to Rafael. I felt cheated and asked him to insist on getting a jacket from the FARC so that Victor could return mine. But he already had Victor's new jacket, and that was all he cared about.

A few nights later, I heard Manuel yell to Victor for help. Rafael was having an epileptic seizure. Victor ran to Sandra's tent in search of something to give him and was lucky to find a syringe and the appropriate medication. Rafael was feeling better the next day.

Chapter 15

GUERRILLEROS AND THEIR PSYCHES

Seven guerrilleros were guarding our group to make sure we didn't escape. They referred to us as 'merchandise' or 'cuchos'. 'Cucho' is a degrading, Colombian term used to address old people. It means something like 'old fogie'.

There were two girls; Sandra and Raquel, ages 16 and 28, five men; Simón, William, Goyo and Faber, whose ages ranged from 15 to 25, and Alacrán (Scorpion), who was about 30.

Simón, the chief, was the only one with a radio phone. He was constantly calling his boss at 'La Compañia', the main FARC headquarters we had passed on our way to the camp. I can still hear his unpleasant voice squawking in my ears—AArrrrrr, me copia?" (Arrrrrr, Ya git it?)

His missing teeth didn't make his diabolical smile any more attractive. Sometimes he tried to be nice and told us our medicines, blankets, boots, jackets, or whatever we needed, were on their way. Occasionally, I felt so helpless I took his word for it.

One day Simón asked me how much I paid the people who worked on my farm. When I told him he said, "If they sign a peace treaty, I'm gonna go work for ya. But there ain't neva gonna be peace in C'lombia".

"Sure you will . . . ," I thought to myself.

Sandra was a pretty little girl with the face of an angel and a permanently stuffed nose. She probably had a broken nose bridge that made it difficult to understand her when she spoke. She turned seventeen during my captivity. Sometimes Sandra would be friendly, but most of the time she ignored my "buenos días". I suspect she had to harden herself to survive; it was easier to be unpleasant in order to avoid closeness that could eventually cause pain.

One day Sandra invited me to visit her tent. It was similar to mine with some basic additions such as clothes hangers for her uniforms, two warm jackets, and two bags of candies, Kool-aids, a few cans of tuna-fish, a comb, a mirror, Pond's cream, a pistol, a shotgun, and lots of ammunition.

Her most valued treasure, which I truly envied, was a 'toldillo'; a small, mesh lining that fits inside the camouflaged tent to break the wind and protect the user from crawling animals. Unfortunately, these 'toldillos' were a luxury reserved only for the 'guerrilleros'.

Sandra and I sat on the straw while she told me about her family, "Ma mom is mean as hell. She was always hittin' me with a belt. When I's twelve, a guy asked if I wanna go to the FARC with him, and I ran away."

Sandra had six siblings; her oldest sister had been stabbed to death at the age of sixteen, shortly before Sandra left home. She resented her mother's indifferent reaction, "All ma mom said was, I told her not ta go ta Bogotá." She was cleaning her pistol while we talked.

"First time I' killed a guy, I's twelve. Damn, I neva wanna do it—I even cried. Ma comandante was testing ma guts and ordered me ta shoot Chepe. Chepe was a guy in ma group. He cried'nd begged me not ta shoot him. Boss told another guerrillero ta shoot both Chepe'n me if I didn't kill Chepe. I crossed ma'self, shot Chepe'n his face, and ran away ta my tent. I've don 'away wit other guys since, but only in battle."

"When they're dying they make funny faces and finally lie still. Real cool!", she calmly remarked.

Sandra had a scar on her breast where a bullet had grazed her. She seemed very proud of it and always managed to leave her shirt open so it could be seen. The freezing wind didn't seem to bother her; she wanted that scar out in the open.

Like the others, she couldn't even read or write. Nevertheless, she was the 'nurse' of the group and kept a plastic bag with some medicine in Simon's tent. She applied injections and other remedies at her own discretion. I prayed to God that I would never need Sandra's 'professional care'.

The girls' duties included keeping the male 'guerrilleros' sexually satisfied. Sometimes other FARC rebels passing through stopped to have a turn with them. Sandra seemed proud of her role as a sexual object and told me she actually enjoyed some of her partners. Her expression changed when she told me that Alacrán, and some of the older men who visited her tent were brutal and mistreated her when she performed her duties. She said, "Lucky I'm gittin' old now. I'll be seventeen and they like ta fuck the little ones, ten or twelve." I felt sorry for her. She was so young and there was such emptiness in her soul

Supposedly, there are no homosexuals among the subversives; it´s said they are shot when they are discovered. If a girl gets pregnant, she is forced to have an abortion. None of my companions revealed that they had been sexually molested but it is known that not only the young, enlisted FARC girls are abused by the bandits, but some of the young, kidnapped women are sometimes raped.

William, age 24, was a strong young man. His head was shaped like the head of an ape and his flat narrow forehead was almost horizontal, framed by straight, black hair. Aside from Sandra, he was the only occasionally civil person in the group 'caring for us'. His false teeth protruded when he smiled.

Once, William came to my tent to chat. He told me he had left his wife and three kids to enlist in the FARC six years before. His oldest son was born when he was fifteen. When I asked if he missed his family, he showed me a photo and told me he never expected to see them again. William joined us for prayer on a few occasions.

He told me, "When a 'guerrillero' enlists, he or she will never be able to leave the FARC alive. Anyone who tries to escape is shot for treason." The term they use when someone is sentenced to death is 'ajusticiar', which means 'bring to justice'. The only way a 'guerrillero' will be allowed to leave the FARC alive is if he is crippled and no longer useful to them.

Alacrán, (Scorpion) about 30 years old. He was the second in command at the camp, but surely the oldest and meanest. He said he had a family, but like the others, had never called them in the seven years he was enlisted. He proudly announced that during his civilian life he had been a tailor and a saddle maker.

Alacrán's main duty was to supervise the others, keep control of the food, and punish the misconduct of both the kidnapped and the bandits. He was the one we asked for permission to bathe or to go to the 'chonto', and he would then order one of the rebels on duty to go along to watch us. The fellow assigned to this duty was called the 'recepcionista' (receptionist) for the day. Alacrán was especially hostile and hardly spoke to any of the captives. There was something very strange and evil about his demeanor, and his expression gave me the chills. We suspected he was a criminal on the run.

One day, as I was passing by Alacran's tent, I heard him instructing the others, "Ya need ta learn how to catch them MF-#$%@&*s on a road. They drive expensive cars, like a Ford or so, and ya have ta act real fast. Ya kick'ém in the balls, press yar gun on their ear and tie'em up. If they say they ain't got no money, just turn'em upside down, shake them, and watch the dough drop out. Otherwise, just shoot'em."

Raquel was a rude, ugly, toothless woman, about 28 years old. Her vocabulary was filthy, and her squeaky voice, offensive. She 'bragged' with a no-fear attitude about "giving any damn #$%@&* his final thrust" whenever it was necessary. She had a pair of scissors, and one of her duties was to cut everybody's hair. I decided to do everything in my power never to put my head in her hands.

Strangely enough, when Raquel cooked, the food tasted a little better than usual. She was always in a hurry to get the meals over with. Breakfast was at 6:00 a.m., lunch at ll:30 a.m. and dinner at 5:00 p.m. When one of us didn't get there immediately, with our beaten up aluminum pot in hand, she yelled, "This ain't no hotel nor your mfwhore house!"

Goyo, 17, was a good-looking boy who never spoke. He had a crush on Raquel and moved into her tent. When she had sex with the others, Goyo waited patiently outside in the cold. According to guerrilla 'protocol', it wasn't considered in 'good taste' to express jealousy.

Faber was fifteen. I was mistaken when I thought he wasn't yet totally corrupted. He had the beautiful smile of a five-year old, but Alacrán was training him to become even meaner than the others. When Faber was ten, his mother gave him to the FARC because the man she lived with didn't want him around. I noticed a big scar on his hand and asked if he was wounded in battle. He said, "No, I's cleanin ma pistol and it went off".

Faber was always picking on me and giving me nasty orders such as, "Y're a shitty pig! I command ya ta go'nd wash yar f . . . jacket rite now—I say this minute, or ya'll end up in one of them holes in the ground!"

The 'guerilleros' from other camps didn't seem to be quite as mean as those in ours´. One day, when three of them were passing by, I smiled and said, "Hi". They gave me a little pack of cookies that I shared with my companions. At that point, I truly appreciated any friendly gesture, no matter who it was from.

We were expected to say "good morning" to each of our captors every day. Of course none of them responded. On one of the occasions when my enormous boots got stuck in the mud, and I struggled to get free, my foot slipped out and landed directly in the deep, cold sludge. Five of our captors were only about ten feet away when I asked if someone could please help me. Not one of them moved. Instead, they all began to sing very loudly. Fortunately, I had my cane and managed to keep my balance until Manuel came to my rescue.

It took me a while to see things objectively, but it really wasn´t difficult to understand why these 'children' were so hateful towards anyone who had a better life than theirs. It wasn't entirely their fault. Coming from extreme poverty and deprivation, most of them hadn't experienced a childhood of affection and parental guidance. Abused by their families, they were easy to recruit and some of them were rounded up by force. Once they were in the movement, the old timers toughened them up and became their role models. They were poisoned with hatred and indoctrinated with a twisted concept of right and wrong. Coming from utter hopelessness into the guerilla army, deprived them of contact with any other reality except the limited times when they watched TV at the Compañia. Their ambition to learn anything constructive, earn honest money, or live in a civilized town or city, had been taken from them.

It was clear that these young rebels, who held temporary power over us, lived terrible lives. They were as captive as we were. Their living conditions were as deplorable as ours, and they ate the same gross food day in and day out. The main difference between us was that we had hope and they didn't. We never lost our faith in God, believing that someday we would return to our families and our normal way of life. They, on the other hand, had nothing to look forward to and their only inspiration was to feel 'powerful' by degrading others.

Sometimes, when I passed by his tent, I heard the 'comandante' reading out loud, syllable-by-syllable, like a first-grader. With youngsters so void of education, I wondered how the FARC became so powerful. They don't want peace because they aren't prepared to hold a normal job or live normal lives. They say there will never be peace in Colombia.

Our captors worked hard only two days a week when they had to cut and bring firewood to the camp to cook the next day. The girls were petite but they worked as hard as the men. I never heard them complain.

On their search for firewood, they caused untold damage to the sparse native trees and shrubs in the nearby area, leaving a mess behind. They had no scruples; Goyo and Faber killed birds for fun with a sling-shot and left them there, on the ground.

They spent most of the time loafing or fooling around. If they weren´t sleeping, they were playing rough games, chasing one another and giving free reign to their naturally, brutal tendencies. Their games were 'anything goes'; biting, scratching, pulling hair and hitting each other below the belt. It was no wonder they ended up with deep, bleeding scratches on their faces, bruises, black eyes, broken noses and knocked-out teeth. These things were bound to happen in a day of fun and games and if they got mad, it wouldn´t have been surprising for them to turn wild, and murder their opponent in cold blood.

Though their commanders forbid it, our guards spent most of their free time playing cards. Being young and unimportant in the guerilla ranks, they didn't have to live up to many rules. I never met anyone who was influential in the FARC during the time of my abduction. The big-shots are usually in their fifties and sixties. The 'supreme commander' of the FARC, Tirofijo, was in his early eighties and never learned to read or write. Nevertheless, they were vehement about taking over the Colombian Government.

Upon further contemplation of this scenario, we couldn't help amusing ourselves with our own imaginary elections, creating a ticket of 'government officials' based on the excellent selection of candidates available to us.

We unanimously voted for Simón as President of Colombia, and William (Smiley) would be his Prime Minister. Who else but evil Alacrán should be the Minister of War and Defense? Sandra, with her nursing abilities, was of course assigned to be Minister of Public Health. Goyo, with his social skills, would be perfect as the Minister of Foreign Affairs, and who was more appropriate than the foul-mouthed Raquel to be the Minister of Cultural Development? Wouldn't this be a perfect governmental cabinet?

Meanwhile, in Bogotá:

A strange man phoned David, and told him he had 'found' a grandmother who is a member of our family. When word spreads around that someone has been kidnapped, there are groups of other bandits that try to collect the ransom even if the victim isn´t in their possession. Sometimes they get away with it. If that happens, the family has to start all over and negotiate with the victim's real kidnappers.

The person who called David told him that he wanted to solve this matter 'rapidito' (fast), and would settle for $30.000.000 pesos ($10,000 dollars). The Comité knew the real kidnappers would be demanding much more, so it was clearly a bluff. In order to sort out the real kidnappers from the impostors, the Comité instructed David to ask whoever called to repeat the names of my grandparents as proof of my identity.

Simón, came to my tent with a pencil and paper and told me my sons needed this information. I wrote down their four, unusual Austrian and Czeck names, and the FARC negotiator called David back with the correct information. The Comité could then rest assured that I was truly under the claws of the FARC and the process could go to the next level.

Soon, an individual who identified himself as Charlie called David on his cell phone on behalf of the FARC. He told David they were holding me under 'economic retention' and stated that if my family ever wanted to see me alive, they would have to pay the FARC the amount of one million US dollars, in cash. At the time, this was the equivalent of three thousand million pesos.

Fortunately, David was prepared. The Comité had decided that he should not identify himself as my son, but rather as a friend the family had assigned to negotiate with them. Charlie was the only person David should talk to.

David told Charlie he hoped they could stay on good terms and get this matter over with as soon as possible. He asked that I be treated well, and told him I was an old woman in extremely poor health, and needed to take medicine for high blood pressure and osteoarthritis every day. Charlie assured David that, "the FARC provides all the medicine the people in their custody need." My health was of great concern to my sons and became an important factor in the negotiation process.

"The woman is old and very sick and she could easily die on you'se guys. If this negotiation ain't handled quickly, the FARC might not git a cent from her family," David said.

"We know it's a stinkin' rich family. Ya better pay right away, or ya'll be sorry when ya git her back in a black bag," Charlie insisted.

"Hey man, where'd ya get that idea? These guys, like lot'sa folks in Colombia, lost their dough and are in deep shit. They wanna go along with you'all but ya're gonna have ta bring that price down. The old lady still works in her little farm where ya picked her up and hardly makes enough ta live. Hey, you've gotta admit that if these guys were loaded, the old hag wouldn't be breakin'er back'n travelling on such a f . . . road in a clunker."

Chapter 16

THE FLOOD—Fourth Week

Manuel told me his concern about Simón re-routing the brook near the camp, to bring running water closer to the cooking area. From his many years of farming, Manuel knew the danger of tampering with brooks; it could easily bring a flood cascading down on the camp. Manuel tried to warn Simón, but he was ignored.

"Don't cha tell me what ta do, just remember who's the boss!," was Simon's reaction.

The camp sat on a wide, mountain ledge with a steep cliff behind it and a precipice on the other side. Sure enough, during the next heavy rainfall our camp was flooded out. It seemed like the whole mountainside was coming down on us with a deafening roar. If our captors decided to abandon the camp in a hurry, I couldn't possibly keep up with them.

Water was pouring in everywhere and some of the sticks holding up the tents broke loose and swept them off the ground. Everyone's belongings were floating away. I didn't lose anything because I was wearing everything I had. Fortunately, God heard our prayers and stopped the rain after two hours. Had the rainstorm lasted a few hours longer, we would probably have been washed away.

Most of us spent the night huddled together around a little gas stove in the kitchen, where the men slept. Built on a slightly higher level, it was the driest spot in the area. Everybody's body-heat was welcome and this dramatic situation brought us closer to our captors, if only for that night. Our only food that evening and the next day was 'aguapanela' with saltine crumbs.

Two days later, Simón, introduced us to Claudio, the young man assigned to be our new 'comandante'. Simón had been demoted.

Claudio was tall and not bad looking. He didn't seem as crude as the others and we hoped the change would be favorable. Immediately, he called for a meeting. There he was, perched on a boulder on higher ground, with his hands on his hips. He reeked of superiority and wanted to make sure we all knew who was boss! We gathered around him.

"Friends", he said, "Life's gonna be easier for ya from now on, but don'tcha try to escape, cause if ya do, you can be sure we'll find ya, and I have orders ta shoot ya down."

When I showed Claudio the holes in the soles of my boots, he actually ordered a new pair. I was happy my feet wouldn't be wet and cold all the time. Of course the boots were a size 12 and I normally wear a size 8—but who cared about that? He also ordered the 'guerrilleros' to construct a walkway with flat stones to make the 'chonto' easier to reach.

A few days later, while sitting in my tent, Claudio came for a visit. He sat down on the straw facing me and we had an amiable conversation.

"My ma abandoned me and I grew up with another family of farmers. I ran away and the FARC found me and trained me ta fight when I's eleven."

It might be important to be on Claudio's good side. He seemed slightly less uncouth than the others.

"You are a nice young man and deserve a much better life. I'm sure you could find a good young wife, only for yourself, work on a farm, and start your own family," I said.

Maybe I should have minded my business, but I thought a friendly conversation might motivate him to improve our living conditions. Perhaps my words would help him look forward to a peaceful life.

"There'll never be peace in Colombia", he said, "but if there is, I wanna marry yar daughter".

When I told him I don't have a daughter, he said: "But ya must have a granddaughter".

"Surely I do—But my oldest granddaughter is only eight".

"That's O.K.—I can wait for her a year or two".

I wasn't expecting such an answer! It bewildered and infuriated me that such a person would be interested in my precious baby. I simply ignored his comment.

Chapter 17

A DREADFUL HIKE

Our captors were planning to bring in more hostages but the campground was covered with so much mud, there was no space to set up other tents.

Three days after the flood, we noticed Faber and William emptying a pot of cooked rice from the day before, into a plastic bag. Manuel told me to get ready. This was a sign we were moving on to another location. He said the bag of cold rice was the only food we would get on our long hike.

His words were confirmed a few minutes later by Claudio, "Pack yar things—we're leavin immediately." Then he called Blanca aside and told her to get ready, she was going home. Blanca came running to our tent.

"Myriam, God heard our prayers! I'm going home!" She was crying for joy.

"You'll be there for your daughter and the baby after all!" We embraced and cried. I was so happy for her and also, it was wonderful to see things moving forward. I gave her the note to my sons and she promised to deliver it to David, in person.

My note read, "My beloved children, I'm adapting and know that you are doing everything in your power to end this nightmare soon. Please ask Dr. Charry what medicine I need, and send it with two sweaters, thermal underwear, warm pajamas, a heavy blanket and a towel. David, darling, the FARC know about your Van. PLEASE SELL IT. Three young men who are here with me were kidnapped when they were traveling in Vans. Also, please stop traveling to 'La Primavera' every weekend—it is very dangerous. I'm sure you are taking good care of Mutti. God bless all of you. I love you so much and pray that soon we will be together. 1000 Hugs & kisses from your Omi."

Blanca was the first person to be released in the past two months. That evening we prayed especially for her safe journey home.

I was afraid of the long hike ahead, but Manuel and Federico assured me I could count on them if I had a hard time keeping up with the group. Manuel helped me take my tent down, fold it and pack it in a sack with my two little blankets and a few things Blanca left me. We were ready immediately.

We set off down the mountain, on foot, towards the river. It was around nine a.m. As usual, it was drizzling. After about four hours of steady walking, we heard a strange noise growing louder and louder until it was a deafening roar. It was what we all feared, an Army helicopter approaching from the mountains behind us. Everyone started running. The heavy sack on my back hampered my progress and I looked around for help. Federico immediately took it from me, and attached it to his backpack. Once I was free from the weight, I was able to run as fast as the rest.

As the helicopter came closer, something fired from above and violently burst on the ground. Everything around us, stones, earth, and vegetation turned upside-down. The force of the explosion threw us down. We were sprawled out in all directions, lying there in a state of shock and confusion, until we slowly started to get up and check around to see who had been wounded.

Goyo, the young bandit, had a big wound on his left leg and was bleeding profusely. Claudio called his superior to report the situation and was given instructions to keep on going with the rest of the group. They would send for Goyo later. Benjamín, our oldest companion, was exhausted. He begged Claudio to let him stay with Goyo, and be picked up later on. Alacrán had a short conversation with Claudio and stayed behind with Benjamín and Goyo. We said good-bye to Benjamín and told him we would see him soon, in Bogotá.

Federico gave me his hand and told me I needed to stay close to him. We were dressed in guerrilla uniforms but the soldiers in the helicopter must have noticed that some of us were hostages and withdrew into the sky. We were happy to see the helicopter leave.

We had orders to keep on running. We ran until some of us had to stop and rest. As soon as Benjamín and Goyo were out of our sight, we heard a few shots. A few minutes later, Alacrán caught up with us and coldly stated, "That old #$%@&* 'cucho' will never f . . . us over again!"

I noticed Benjamin's ring on this cold-blooded, murderer's finger and knew the shots we heard had killed Benjamín and maybe even Goyo. Something snapped inside me and my fear of those scoundrels turned to rage.

I lost control and grabbed him by his neck, yelling hysterically, "You miserable coward! You murderer! I wouldn't mind dying as long as you die too!" When he recovered from his surprise, a look of cruel sarcasm spread across his face as he reached for his gun.

Victor, Federico and Manuel, with tears in their eyes, calmed me down and begged Alacran not to shoot. They had been through similar situations and understood how I felt. "You've been so brave, you can't give up now!" they said. Eventually, my anger subsided and I realized that losing control would put my life in danger.

We had to keep walking very fast and only stopped occasionally to drink water from the brook. I couldn't get poor Benjamín off my mind. My only comfort was that he would now be spared from whatever else was coming our way.

The night was black when we finally stopped to rest on some rocks. I was full of anguish and distress after that atrocious day and cried myself to sleep on Federico's shoulder. In the morning, we ate some cold rice from the big plastic bag with our bare, dirty hands and continued our wretched journey as soon as it was daylight. Our destination wasn't far and after about two hours of fast walking, we arrived. What would this new camp hold for us?

Chapter 18

ADJUSTING TO THE SECOND CAMP

The new camp was also located above the timber line where only sparse vegetation can survive. These mountaintops, that appear to be so beautiful and majestic from a distance, are not fit for human life. And the circling hawks watched from above.

The decaying ruins around us indicated that another camp had been there recently. The wooden logs that gave shape to our familiar 'beds' were lying in the mud, filled with soaked straw. After removing the rotten straw, my companions set up the camouflaged material they called "tents" to cover the 'beds' and cut long, heavy grass to fill them. Each bed was wide enough for two people. They set mine up last. It was somewhat narrower than the others.

Rafael, with his customary air of self-assurance, stated that my tent was going to be the 'caleta de los abuelos' (grandma and grandpa's hideaway).

He told them to make the bed wider, and in case anyone missed his intention he said, "From now on, I'll sleep with her."

I didn't make a fuss about Rafael's arrogant statement and calmly asked Claudio to, "Please leave the bed narrow—I will sleep alone."

Later, my friends kiddingly asked me if I wasn't delighted by such a flattering offer. Rafael kept telling me, "We´ll be so happy when we are a real couple and we can travel to the United States together." He often volunteered non-requested information such as, "Good thing I don't need Viagra."

Rafael's advances were ridiculous and got on my nerves. He was exactly the type of man I dislike—an unreliable, braggart, always trying to take advantage of someone else. What he really wanted was someone to wait on him and wash his clothes. My response to Rafael was always the same, "Your wife and son are waiting for you."

In contrast, my other companions were the kind of friends you could count on. Together, we fought to overcome our depression by maintaining conversations that provided a balance to our unhappy, daily lives. We talked about a wide range of subjects and experiences, including our travels, or simple gossip about friends and relatives. We felt free to share about things we probably wouldn´t have discussed under different circumstances, such as sex and politics. Sometimes we compared customs that were strange to us and talked about human behavior in faraway places. Manuel and Victor would even come forth with a joke or two when they were in good spirits.

Manuel told us that he was a national 'coleo' champion; a typical sport from the Colombian 'Llanos Orientales' (Eastern plains). The goal of a 'coleo cowboy' is to bring a wild bull under control with his bare hands. It takes a daring expert to even try such a feat. The bull is released a few seconds ahead of his adversary, the man on horseback. When the horse and 'coleador' catch up with the bull, the man grabs the bull's tail and spurs the horse forward. The skill lies in speeding up the horse and twisting the bull's tail, knocking the beast on its back with its legs in the air. The 'coleador' that takes the bull down the fastest, is the winner.

Coleo tournaments are accompanied by a typical barbecue of the region. It made me drool to remember the exquisite 'Ternera a la Llanera' (barbecued veal) and 'Chiguiro' (wild pig) I had eaten when I visited the Llanos Orientales with my parents as a child.

I told them one of my most treasured memories about one of my trips to Vienna, "On summer evenings, people go to the Stadt Park to attend a beautiful, Waltz concert performed by a national orchestra. A group of young couples unexpectedly stroll out of the woods and do a stunning, Waltz exhibition. The men dress in 'frack' (tails) and the ladies in long, pastel colored gowns. After their performance, each dancer invites someone from the audience on to the dance floor. In no time, everybody is waltzing, swept away by the magic of the evening." My description transported us away from our misery for a little while. We could almost hear the music and visualize the dancers spinning around.

Federico came up with the story of his friend's father: "He was a worker at the farm of a rich man," he said, "and he had a pretty daughter that was reaching her fifteenth birthday, the age to be married. Their parents had decided she would marry the son of another worker. As tradition had it, a few days before the wedding the bride's father's 'Patron' should perform his 'derecho de pernada'—his right and his duty.

"What's the Derecho de Pernada?" asked Pedro.

"Up until the third decade of the twentieth century, the 'patron' had the 'privilege' of deflowering his workers' daughters shortly before they married. It was then the girl's honor to bear him a child. These children had certain privileges because they were brought up in well-to-do surroundings, shared their childhood with many half-brothers and half-sisters, and were offered a good education."

"The girl I knew went ahead and married the boy assigned to her by her parents, and her first child was protected by the Patron," Federico continued.

Although this custom sounded strange and even repulsive, I had to admit there were some benefits that came with it.

We daydreamed about traveling to the Rio de Janeiro Carnival, and the men fantasized about attending a Samba session where attractive, skimpily dressed 'garottas' (girls) invited them to dance. At other times we paid an imaginary visit to a'Tablao Flamenco' (Flamenco Dance Show) in Spain.

Some of my friends missed the soap operas on the local TV channels like '*Café*' (Coffee) and 'Pero Sigo Siendo el Rey' (I'm still the King), a big hit in most Spanish-speaking countries. Every time someone new arrived at the camp, some of us inquired about what was happening with 'Betty la Fea' (Ugly Betty), the most applauded Colombian soap opera of the decade. It has been translated to many languages.

These conversations were a healthy escape and renewed our hope. One of us would always come up with a story or memory to hold the group's interest.

From time to time, we would check to see if there was a 'guerrillero' snooping around outside the tent. Our conversations were quite personal. At times we were making plans for the future, even though we knew there might not be a future for some of us.

Federico, Manuel, and Victor reminded me of my sons. They were concerned about my welfare at all times, and I felt protected. To alleviate my worries Federico would say, "Myriam, remember that we are in a 0-star hotel, and need to be patient. If our negotiator is smart and we stay long enough, our bill (meaning the ransom) will be lower—and hopefully, affordable to our families".

Life in the second camp was similar to the first one. The only difference was the cooking and eating area—the 'rancha'. It was a hole dug in the ground somewhat bigger than a king-size bed and about four to five feet deep. Sandra and William drained out the rainwater and covered the 'rancha' with a canvas.

Alacrán and Faber provided two forked branches to support the stick where they hung two pots over the fire. To step in and out of the 'rancha' we had to descend four steep, slippery steps of mud. I told Claudio that I was afraid to slip and fall when stepping into the hole, and asked him to let me stay outside and just hand my pot over to the person who was serving. His answer was, "NO".

Farther down the same mountainside, about a block away, were five coffin-shaped holes full of water. Sandra drained one of them to use for garbage. When I asked William the purpose of the other holes he answered, in a very matter-of-fact way, "We alw's dig graves so we'r ready—ya neva know when we'l need'em! Yarself might end up in one of'em!" When I had to walk down there to throw the food I hadn't eaten in the garbage, I had the ghastly feeling one of those graves was waiting for me.

I asked if they could please serve me very small portions so I wouldn't have to go down there so often. They continued to fill my pot to the brim, "just for discipline". There wasn't a dry spot or log to sit on so we stood together in a group while we ate our meals. When it was raining hard, I ate in my tent.

To liven things up, we fantasized about our meager meals.

"Isn't this chicken cacciatore delicious?"

"Yes, but the barbequed steak and vegetables we had yesterday were even better".

Or, while eating those disgusting 'cancharinas', "Isn't this four-cheese pizza exquisite?"

The monotony was abruptly broken when William appeared with a big slab of ribs covering his head and back, dripping blood all over his shoulders.

Every month, the FARC killed a cow they stole, and distributed the meat among the nine camps. The meat was heavily salted to keep it from rotting.

However, it was only for the 'guerrilleros'. If we were lucky, they'd throw us some fat and bone.

One day William sneaked us a tiny pack of 'frunas' (chewy candy) and we each got one. I hadn't had a piece of candy in months, but this delicious, sticky little 'fruna' ended up in the cavity of a huge filling I had lost from one of my molars, and there wasn't an aspirin or any other painkiller available. I was expecting a toothache to start up any minute.

The 'chonto' in this camp was much farther from our tents. To get there, we had to walk about three blocks in the mud, jump over two brooks, and to make matters worse, it was right next to the main pathway leading away from the area. Sometimes rebels from other camps passed by while one of us was busy at the 'chonto'.

After one of these embarrassing encounters Carlos told us, "Can you believe that when I was crouching there yesterday a bunch of bandits passed by and ran over to greet me? Two of them even embraced me and then one of them pushed me right into the 'chonto'."

During the first afternoon at the new camp, Claudio sent Sandra to show us to the river where we were to bathe and do our laundry. We had to walk down a steep mountain and across a big swamp. It was impossible not to sink into the deep mud. Going down to the river was difficult enough, but climbing back up was exhausting. The first time I made that climb I was out of breath and my heart began to beat violently. I fainted again. When I awoke, I heard Victor asking Claudio to assign the older people a place closer to the camp. He was reluctant, but after a long debate he had Sandra lead us to another spot we named, "Methuselah's Pond".

MEANWHILE, IN BOGOTÁ:

Blanca called my ex-husband, Hernando, to deliver the note I had so carefully written that listed my needs. It was unusual, but Charlie had left a phone number for David to contact him as soon as he could round up the money to pay my ransom, and David was eager to contact Charlie regarding my list of needs.

Captain Perez, the committee chairman, had Charlie's contact number traced and believe it or not, he turned out to be a school teacher from a small town in the middle of nowhere. This indicated how the FARC had infiltrated all walks of life. It was the number of the only grocery store in the town, and the only phone located in that small community.

Part of the strategy was to make friends with Sonia, the woman who usually answered the phone, so she would call Charlie whenever David needed to talk to him. When Sonia told David that her husband needed medical attention, he suggested she bring the man to Bogotá and offered to help them contact a doctor. She never called back.

During one of their conversations, David insisted to Charlie about getting a package to me and Charlie accepted, adding, "Make sure ya send me perfumes for ma ladies. Hey bro, and remember I git drunk on Black Label Scotch Whiskey. I'll git back ta ya soon ta let'çha know how ta send all that shit".

David and Ricardo followed his instructions in full detail. They prepared a back-pack containing everything I had listed and added two bottles of whisky and some cheap perfumes. David wrote a note to Charlie about getting it to me as soon as possible and gave it to the driver of the bus Charlie had indicated. Charlie confirmed he had received it. However, my needs were unimportant to the FARC and they were never delivered to me.

Chapter 19

KEEPING MY SPIRITS UP

I COULDN'T LET the sadness defeat me. There were so many things I wanted to do, places to visit and people to meet! In my youth, I enjoyed writing 'coplas,' which are short musical rhymes giving a humorous twist to a person or a current event. I was out of practice and didn't even have a pencil and paper to write them down, but sometimes, while trying to fall asleep, the day's happenings would come to my mind in this form, flowing without effort. Usually 'coplas' are accompanied by Colombian folkloric music called, "Guabina Chiquinquireña". Once I started, many 'coplas' would flood into my mind and amuse me for a while. Of course, the English translation might not rhyme:

> "Los viejitos nos bañamos en
> el Pozo Matusalén
> que tiene una gran ventaja
> de todos lados lo ven."

"We old folks get to bathe
down at Mathuselah's pond
The best part is
You'll be seen from near'nd 'yond."

————

"Ese Victor es Doctor
de primera calidad
pero lo mejor que tiene
es su voto de fidelidad"

"Victor is a Doctor
of the highest quality
and his test of character is,
his vow of fidelity."

————

"Gloria ponte feliz
ya vuelve tu Federico;
de la panza que traía
no queda ni'el recuerdito"

"Cheer up Gloria dear,
Your Federico's coming home,
It's no time to fear,
his potbelly's almost gone."

———

"Manuel siempre ha sido
el angel de los viejitos;
pero no hay que'xagerar
pues se pone berriondito"

"T'old folks Manuel´s been
an angel through and through
but sometimes he gets mad
and takes it out on you."

One day Carlos, who was 66, went down to the river to do his laundry. When he returned he told us, "Guess what, Sandra, who was on duty, took off all her clothes and bathed right next to me?" This surely warmed our friend Carlos up!

"Carlitos se bajo'al río
a lavar su pantalón.
Sandra lo pilló y le'hizo
Su buena demostración."

"Carlos went down to the river
To wash his underwear
Sandra ain´t just no swimmer
Wow! At least he got a stare."

———

"De sus picardías se'acuerda
Nuestro amigo Rafaelito
paz y'amor ha d'encontrar
con Carmenza'y su Pepito."

"Rafael's always proud,
of his past shenanigans,
But h'll only find love'n peace,
with his wife'n son again."

———

"En la caleta de Sandra
se'oye siempre jugarreta
Ojo niña no'vaya'ser
que te'agarren una teta".

"In Sandra's cozy tent
the guys play'n wrestle
Watch'out girl or you gonna
find your tits´r in a tussle."

Before dawn, I always checked for those disgusting, hairy black worms in the straw. Then I followed my usual routine: massaging my freezing feet and blowing on my hands in a feeble attempt to warm them up. The next step was to put on as many socks as possible, folding the two longest ones back over my feet for an additional layer.

There was no source of light and heat. My candle was useless without a lighter, and humidity made it impossible to light the few matches available. Blanca had left me her flashlight, but there were no batteries in the camp. "Maybe next week", was always Claudio's answer.

One night Raquel shone her flashlight in my face to wake me up, "Hey, what's the time?"

"Sorry, Raquel, but I can't see my watch in the dark".

"Don't ya git smart with me ya old bitch. Git out here and lemme see that #p&°!&$ watch o'yars. And be happy I don't shoot ya this time. Next time ya'r not respectful, I will!" That's what I admired about Raquel—her kindness and delicate manners! I wanted to slap her but I had to get up anyway and show her my watch—she was pointing her gun in my face.

I needed God's help to face those long, cold and often sleepless nights. At times, I would let my mind wander back to my fondest memories; things I hadn't remembered in many years. This helped me maintain my sanity and drift peacefully off to sleep.

Chapter 20

RIVER BOAT

ON ONE OF those nights, my mind wandered back to the mid-fifties when I was thirteen. My brother Martin had invited Luke, one of his friends from Princeton to spend a vacation with us. Whenever we had foreign visitors my parents planned something interesting to make their experience in Colombia memorable. On this occasion they arranged for a boat trip down the Magdalena River to the city of Barranquilla, Colombia's main port on the Atlantic Ocean.

The Atlántico, our ship of eighty passengers, was old and rustic. We travelled in the company of a twin ship called David Arango. They were similar to the steam paddle wheelers on the Mississippi River. Every evening the two ships docked at some small port along the river and we enjoyed a Colombian style celebration with live music, provided by local town musicians, and a dancing party for the passengers on the main deck. Such evenings turned into big events for the little towns' people, who came from far and wide to sell their handicrafts to the passengers.

The source of the Magdalena River is in the Andes mountain-range and it flows through the central area of Colombia, cutting through dense jungles before it empties into the Atlantic Ocean. The breath-taking sunrises and exotic jungle concerts performed by mysterious birds and wild animals, created a delightful and picturesque journey. While the ship was moving, the breeze kept us comfortable but it was stifling hot when we docked.

Every so often, the captain appeared on deck with a long stick and measured the depth of the river to avoid the shallow places where the Atlántico might go aground. I was fascinated by his dexterity with the measuring stick and had never seen anyone quite like this enormous, round, good-natured, whimsical black man, the best dancer his size I have ever seen!

Two young American ladies that were teachers at the American school in Barranquilla, boarded the Atlántico at the port of Puerto Berrío. This made the journey much more enjoyable for Martin and Luke, who had a great time spending late nights on the deck, dancing and drinking Uva Postobón, (a grape flavoured soda) and rum.

On one corner of the cargo deck was a collection of cages containing about eighty monkeys of various species that were on their way to the Atlantic coast to be exported to zoos in the United States. There were also several big cages with beautiful, tropical birds and colourful 'guacamayos' (macaws) sitting on the freight deck.

Apparently, someone who thought it would be amusing to let the monkeys go free, opened their cages before daybreak. That morning, we woke up to a monkey invasion! They were everywhere! The kitchen was of course their favorite spot and soon everything in it was upside down—a disaster! Amidst delighted screeches, the monkeys managed to eat all the food. They soiled the floors, walls, pots, kitchenware, and everything in sight. The Captain yelled, "Holy cow, there's shit everywhere!"

He invited all passengers to an abundant meal of Colombian 'tamales' at a restaurant in the next port, so the crew could clean up the mess. It was both comical and tragic to watch the sailors chase the monkeys, trying to get them back into their cages. Many of them jumped into the river and swam towards the jungle. Sad to say, some of them drowned, but it was rewarding to see how others reached their freedom!

The sound of airplanes flying over the area drew me back into my cruel reality. Every time I heard a plane, I hoped it was the Army coming to our rescue. On the other hand, I was scared to be caught in the middle of another confrontation.

Colombia had literally turned into a war zone and our economy was in shreds. Every time the Army managed to surround one of the guerrilla groups and was on the verge of carrying out its duty, they received a mysterious command from the Government ordering them to stop the operation and let the 'guerrilleros' go. This happened again and again for many years, under the command of different governments. The Colombian Army was finally properly equipped and trained. Why were the FARC villains allowed to get away with their criminal actions that caused so much grief and destruction?

Chapter 21

SAD MEMORIES

Carlos brought up a conversation about the "Bogotazo". This was a revolution that occurred on April 9, 1948, as a consequence of the hatred between Liberals and Conservatives, the two existing political parties that were killing each other on sight. I was eleven at the time.

It was triggered by the murder of Jorge Eliécer Gaitán, the Liberal leader, who was shot while entering a restaurant in Bogotá. When word of his death got out, the people rioted with fury, committing terrible acts of vandalism. I clearly remember two trucks stacked with corpses passing by our house.

Downtown, near my Dad's office, the mob lit an enormous fire. I'll never forget how panic stricken we were while waiting for Vatti to get home. Finally he arrived, crying. I heard him tell Mutti that during his six hour walk from the office, he saw four grown-ups and two children murdered on the streets. The mobs were burning buildings and cars, vandalizing stores, and stealing everything they could get their hands on.

It was too dangerous to stay on our beds with flying bullets outside that could easily come in through a window, so we all cuddled up together on the floor that night.

Back to our sad reality, Carlos said, "You young guys were lucky you hadn't been born. Those years of "Violencia" were hellish, especially for us peasants. It was a bloody war between 'Chulavitas' (Conservatives) and 'Cachiporros' (Liberals). Both parties were brutal. They were capable of arriving at a farm or town, and massacring a whole family or anybody else who happened to be there, just because they were from the other party. The Conservatives wanted a traditional government with one strong leader that would remain loyal to Roman Catholic beliefs, while the Liberals wanted to separate the State from the Church. Most people didn't even know the difference between them.

"I remember the night my parents rushed us out to hide in the jungle," said Pedro. "The mob reached our house a few minutes later. What has haunted me all my life is the memory of the scene we returned to the next day. The bodies of our aunt, uncle and five cousins were spread out all over the house. And these things kept going on, they kept killing each other like animals."

"You're wrong, my friend" I said. "Animals don't usually kill unless they are hungry. Some humans are, by far, the most vicious members of the animal kingdom."

Chapter 22

REMEMBER THE "NARCOS" (DRUGLORDS)

We were all standing around talking after our rice and lentils breakfast when someone made a comment about the drug lords and their influence.

"Do you remember the 80's and 90's, when the "narcos" (drug mafia) were practically ruling the country?" Victor said.

"Yes, I was only a child, but who could possibly forget those awful years?

We lost our best farm because my Mom couldn't resist the pressure some guys put on her to sell it," Manuel said. "Seven heavily armed men drove up in two cars. The trunks of the cars were supposed to be packed with sacks of money. They intimidated Mom until she signed the papers. Then they drove away real fast taking the signed documents and the sacks of money with them. We were lucky and grateful they didn't kill her."

"I have heard of other occasions when the 'mafiosos' stole someone's farm, and then other times when they 'bought' the best lands and the most expensive homes in the country. It was bizarre," Victor said, "Their interior decorators hung up original paintings by famous artists their clients had never even heard of. Most of them had eighteen karat gold fixtures, huge crystal lamps and other extravagances everywhere, even in the bathrooms, kitchens and garages."

"They found a large, solid gold motorcycle in Rodriguez Gacha's farm. He was the second most important drug-dealer of that period (Pablo Escobar was the first). After Escobar was killed, they found many sacks, each containing five million US dollars in cash buried on his land," said Pedro. "There are probably still dozens of sacks packed with millions of dollars buried on the land of other 'mafiosos'."

"They flew in planes of prostitutes for their parties and shoveled out money in all directions," Federico said. "Remember the discotheques they built in the middle of nowhere? Some of them could compare to the fanciest Discos in New York, Rome, or Rio de Janeiro. This was one of their ways to launder money."

"A special jail was built to imprison them; a 'Maximum Security Prison' made to order by Pablo Escobar's own architects that catered to his comfort," he continued. "He came and went any time he desired, and even had a switch next to his bed that controlled the prison's lights."

"And I remember when the Government tried to put an end to these special privileges and extradite the drug lords to the United States, they murdered the Minister of Defense, Rodrigo Lara Bonilla. Then they bombed public buildings, shopping malls and residential areas all over the country," Manuel added.

Everybody who lived in Colombia during those years was affected in some way by the mafia violence. "I was out shopping with my husband one morning," I said, "when suddenly, we heard a terrible explosion. As we approached our building, we saw that the streets in the area were blocked by the Police so we parked the car several blocks away and walked home. Most buildings all around were severely damaged and the streets were covered with debris and broken glass.

"About one third of our building was in ruins. The door-man's body was lying on the floor next to the elevators, and people were carrying the wounded down the stairs. It was tragic! All the windows in the eight-floor building had exploded and there was wreckage everywhere. Somehow we managed to reach the second floor but realized it was hopeless to try and get to our apartment on the seventh floor. We left the building and stayed at my brother's home," I continued. "David was studying Business Administration at the time. Alejandro was in med-school and Ricardo was in his last year of high-school. We had to live part of the time in Buganviles and commute to Bogotá until our building was restored." A downpour of rain interrupted the conversation, scattering us back to our tents.

Chapter 23

ABOUT NARCOTICS IN COLOMBIA

THE NARCOTIC INDUSTRY was born during the Korean War in the 50's, when veterans returned to the United States bringing their addiction to marihuana and heavier narcotics back to their homeland from the jungles of Asia. Under the pressure and horror of war, drugs became a common method of escape for many soldiers, and by the time the Vietnam War came around, the business was flourishing.

For centuries, Perú and Bolivia had wild marihuana and coca plants growing abundantly in their forests. Traditionally, the undernourished natives in those countries chewed coca leaves to appease their hunger and give them more energy to work. Coca plantations were enlarged and new ones were established to make room for the production of limited amounts for the Colombian drug cartels. Raw coca was processed into a final product in hidden labs deep in the Colombian jungles, and then exported to their worldwide contacts. In the 1990s, international efforts shut down the coca plantations in Peru and Bolivia. Colombian drug lords found that raw coca could be successfully cultivated in the rich and fertile lands of Caquetá in the southern Colombian jungles, a perfect habitat. They encouraged hundreds of needy families from all regions in Colombia, even some who had not been farmers before, to move to the jungle areas and farm raw coca as a means of survival.

Soon, other peasants in the far jungle areas found it was easier and more profitable to grow coca and poppy seed than cattle, yucca, plantains, rubber, or other crops they had grown before. The transportation difficulties they had experienced getting their previous harvests to market were easily solved when they decided to grow the basic, raw materials for the manufacture of narcotics. Their produce was picked up and paid for at the farms.

After the arrest and killing of the most well-known drug lords in the middle and late nineties, the more recent leaders have kept a much lower profile than their predecessors, who lived ostentatious lifestyles. The FARC took control of a major part of the drug industry and acquired the title of "Narco-guerrilla".

There is a popular product similar to 'Crack,' made of coca leaves, cement and lime, a mixture that is devastating to the human brain. 'Bazuco' is much cheaper than processed cocaine and is consumed by the young and the poor.

The Colombian people are generally resilient, resourceful, and possess a natural ability for survival. However, at that time the average Colombian tended to suffer from low self-esteem. This was partially due to the fact that the International Press was lowering Colombia's image by seldom mentioning anything good about the country. During those years, when a Colombian passenger exhibited his passport at an airport anywhere around the world, he received disrespectful treatment. The image of Colombia has been changing in the last decade. There are thousands of prestigious Colombians who are currently admired and well liked for their hard work, honesty, friendliness, tenacity and good behaviour.

Chapter 24

MARCELO, ESTELA AND A TERRIFYING NIGHT

We had been at the second camp for a week when early one morning they brought in two new hostages; **Marcelo** and **Estela**, a couple in their late thirties. They were dismayed about their children, an eight year old boy and a little girl, age five.

On the evening they were kidnapped, Marcelo and Estela had left their children at home with a fourteen year old girl who was hired to do their house cleaning and play with them. They were on their way to pick up Estela's mother in a neighboring town to take her for a medical visit and were only going to be away for about three hours when they were abducted.

Estela was a nurse at a factory, and Marcelo an assistant technician at the gas company. They were paying off mortgages on their home, and their old SUV, and could barely make ends meet. Of course, this was the end of their 1982 vehicle. They bought such a big car because no one else in their family owned one and they could squeeze in as many people as possible for a picnic or Sunday ride. They weren't only anxious about their children but were also distressed about losing their jobs. Colombia was suffering a twenty-two percent unemployment rate at the time. This didn't include the thirty-two percent of self-employed people doing chores such as street vending, renting cell-phone minutes, washing and mending clothes, or house cleaning. If someone was lucky enough to have a steady job, he certainly wanted to keep it.

'Comandante' Claudio said, "They're here by mistake. I'll send her back right away, and if these guys really ain't rich, he can go too." Of course this wasn't true. Marcelo and Estela were held for two and a half months until the FARC made sure there wasn't anyone who could pay their ransom.

Alacrán came to my tent and brusquely pulled away my bigger blanket. I was never warm enough, but it had been better than nothing. Now, all I had left was the very small one I had in the shack where I spent the first night.

He was also after a little foam-rubber mat that Blanca had left me. I sat on it in protest, but he poked me violently with his gun, pushed me away, and took the mat.

I was very upset and yelled, "If you plan to kidnap more people, you should at least get enough supplies to take care of them!" Unfortunately, my protest created more problems than I had imagined.

Two of the bandits abruptly took my tent down and set it up next to the coffin-shaped holes. I went into panic and begged Claudio not to do this—but it was useless. I couldn't sleep one minute and spent a horrific night far away from my companions and with the dreadful feeling that I was surrounded by corpses.

The next morning I told Claudio, "If you're planning to leave me there, I beg you to shoot me and get it over with right now!"

Victor heard me and was stunned by my reaction. He warned me never to say such a foolish thing again. He said, "We both know that it would be an everyday accomplishment for Alacrán to shoot you or anyone else."

I had taken a stupid risk, but it worked. Claudio ordered William to set up my tent where it had been before, next to my companions.

"Myriam, you shouldn't be so rebellious," Manuel and Pedro scolded me, "you could get yourself killed!" They were right. I was profoundly rebellious and had never accepted the outrageous idea of submitting to such wild and sinister characters.

The 'guerrilleros' had two decks of ancient cards they lent Manuel from time to time when they weren't playing. Federico, Manuel, Estela, Marcelo and I liked to play Rummy 51, in my tent. The red color of the hearts and diamonds had faded—they were almost invisible and it strained our eyes to figure them out, but we enjoyed having something to keep us busy.

Marcelo had been a physical education trainer. He was a strong man. Estela said that Marcelo was eighty kilos of "pure fiber".

That evening I came up with the following 'copla':

> "Setenta kilos de fibra
> y diez más de corazón,
> mantienen a Estelita
> satisfecha y con tesón".

> "Seventy kilos of fiber
> Plus ten more of heart,
> Keep Estela full of pep
> And singing like a lark."

Another copla about Estela and Marcelo:

"Mucho currucuteo y
uyuyuyes de pasión
S'escuchan por las noches
en la caleta Monzón."

"Oh's, and aah's and love talk
with sighs and sweet passion
come drafting through the air at night
it's the Jamboree Monzón."

The words to this 'copla' weren't really true. They were only meant to distract us from our sadness for a while. My tent was next to theirs and I could hear Marcelo and Estela crying themselves to sleep every night. Their parents were too old and too sick to take care of their grandchildren. Estela was hopeful that her sister might have taken them into her home.

Three months later, when the FARC finally accepted the fact that there was no way to collect any money from their family, they set Marcelo and Estela free, under the condition that they would appear on a TV program and follow a script the FARC had prepared for them.

I called them as soon as I was released and Estela told me, "Instead of escorting us to a town or a road where we could catch a bus to Bogotá, we were sent back on our own and crossed the mountain-range without food, shelter or proper clothing. They didn´t even let us take the rubber boots we wore at the camp. I had to wear the high heels I was wearing when we were kidnapped."

They were fortunate when some soldiers in a helicopter over-flying the area spotted them, picked them up and took them to the nearest air base. When they finally made it home, they were interviewed on TV where they told the world about their 'wonderful and most exciting vacation'.

Chapter 25

PECULIAR HAPPENINGS

Things do happen in Colombia that might seem particularly strange to people in other parts of the world. No wonder Gabriel Garcia Márquez, our Colombian Nobel prize winner, created the 'Magic Realism', so popular in Latin American literature. Here are a few of my own anecdotes illustrating the Colombia's bizarre and chaotic charm.

One day, when traveling with David and my nephew, Jaime, to David's country house on a narrow road, we had a startling experience that could have been fatal, but fortunately we lived to tell the story. Part of this road had been excavated right through a hill. The two remaining sections of the hill rose up about thirty meters on each side. Suddenly, a cow flew off the top of the hill, onto the road. The poor thing was probably out to pasture when she slipped off the cliff, bounced off the hood of Jaime's car, and landed on the road in front of us. At the sight of the "flying cow" Jaime stepped on the brakes and saved us from being crushed.

Needless to say, all four of us, and especially the cow, were in shock! Her flight, however, was perfectly timed so that nobody was badly hurt. After a while, she was able to get up and calmly limp away. The front of the car was severely damaged but the motor was O.K. We turned around and drove back to David's office in Bogotá where we exchanged the car for his Van.

* * * * * *

And there was Doña Rosita, an unforgettable character. She was a tiny, peasant woman about four feet tall, in her early seventies. She lived in a little cottage next to the river, close to Buganviles. Doña Rosita's wrinkled face was framed by two very thin, gray braids, and she greeted me with her almost toothless smile. She wore the typical peasant outfit of a woman her age: a man's black hat, a big black shawl, a long, wide skirt, a blouse and straw slippers tied with black ribbons called 'alpargatas'.

Doña Rosita made a successful career cutting slate stones from the river bed with a sledge—hammer. Her particular expertise was to shape them into the sizes and forms her clients needed. Though this tiny woman didn't have anyone to help her with her heavy labour, she shipped out truckloads of rock. I hadn't seen her for a few months and asked Jaider about Doña Rosita. His answer was,

"Doña Rosita isn't selling stones any more. Now she is a doctor. "What? A doctor? What kind of doctor?"

"You know, one of those doctors who give people massages and put their bones back in place."

* * * * * *

The Principal of the Colombian National University in Bogotá, a young man born of foreign parents, was giving a speech to a large group of students in the University Auditorium. The students weren't paying attention to his energetic speech, and he became very upset. So, what did the Principal do? He turned his back on his audience, pulled down his trousers, and mooned the astonished crowd. He was demoted a few days later.

But here comes the most amazing part of the story. Two weeks after this unusual incident that was in every newspaper around the country and in many other countries as well, our ex-Principal was elected Mayor of Bogotá, the second most important position in the country!

When I returned to Bogotá after three years of absence, I noticed there had been a favorable change in the behavior and attitude of taxi drivers, waiters, policemen, store attendants and employees in service positions.

I was told that our Mayor, who was reelected, organized a mandatory yearly program to train these people in courtesy, good manners, friendliness and efficient customer service. He also passed strict laws to change destructive habits such as drunken driving, ignoring traffic-lights, bars staying open till daylight, and minors being on the street till late hours. It´s interesting that our Mayor and his bride celebrated their marriage ceremony riding on an elephant.

Between his first and second terms, we were lucky to have another young Mayor whose administration was highly beneficial to Bogotá. He transformed our beaten-up city into a modern, livable capital with excellent opportunities for production and international trade. He initiated an efficient public transport system called 'Transmilenio', which has been copied in other cities in Colombia and in several other countries.

Chapter 26

THINGS THAT CAME TO MY MIND

Eventually, I began to accept my pitiful condition and stopped crying so much. But when Mutti's ninety-second birthday came around, I couldn't get her off my mind. I was her only daughter and she was completely dependent on me. I imagined how helpless and lonely she must have been without me. I knew Martin was, as always, visiting her every day, and her grandchildren and caring friends would be sure to accompany her as often as possible. Nevertheless, I was concerned about her health and how my abduction was affecting her.

My thoughts often turned to each of my grandchildren. I hoped no one had told them the truth, they were much too young to understand the meaning of the word 'kidnapped', and it would only create distress in their little minds. I missed their birthdays, little Felipe's first 'crawling' days, and Vicky's first attempts to roller-skate. How I missed our bird-watching and tap-dancing sessions, Valentina and Patty's favorites. And I wouldn't be there to listen to Marcela's adventures at grammar school or play soft-ball with Billy. And who would be 'Raton Perez', the Colombian version of 'Tooth Fairy', when teeth were lost? I wouldn't be there to pick up little Felipe and dance with him to comfort him when he cried, the way I did with my older grand-babies.

I never lost faith that I would survive but I couldn't shake off the macabre stories of what happened to others. The father of a friend was one of the first people to be kidnapped in Colombia back in the early sixties. He knew that if the bandits successfully collected a high ransom, the crime of kidnapping would become 'in fashion', as it did. He made his family promise that if he was ever abducted, they would not pay ransom. As a result, this gentleman was murdered by his captors.

About fifteen years later, the same family was struck by tragedy once again. One of this gentleman's daughters was kidnapped by another guerrilla group. She was a lawyer and directed an institution to protect the rights of indigenous communities. She was a beautiful, kind and lovable woman. This time, the terrorists didn't demand money—they said she was "retained for political reasons". She was tortured, brutally murdered and her pregnant body was dumped on a street in Bogotá.

* * * * * *

In the late sixties, the two year-old baby niece of another dear friend was kidnapped by the FARC. Fortunately this story had a happy ending and the infamy ended when the band of scoundrels was captured. They spent many years in jail. The same little girl is now a prominent physician and lives in Spain.

* * * * * *

Initially, only the richest people were in danger. Gradually, the FARC started abducting people from the press as well as politicians. Then the rich, the famous and even common people were taken almost at random. According to police statistics, eight people were kidnapped in Colombia every day in the late nineties and early two-thousands, giving Colombia the embarrassing title of "Kidnapping Capital of the World".

There is a famous writing by the Lutheran Pastor, Martin Niemoeller, who was imprisoned by the Nazis at Theresienstadt Concentration Camp. It read, "In Germany, the Nazis came for the Socialists. I didn't speak up because I was not a Socialist. Then they came for the Trade Unionists. I didn't speak up because I was not a Trade Unionist. Then they came for the Jews. I didn't speak up because I was not a Jew. Then they came for me. By that time there was nobody left to speak up for me."

This story repeated itself in Colombia.

Chapter 27

COLOMBIA, LAND OF FRUITS AND FLOWERS

COLOMBIANS STICK TO strong, family ethics and believe togetherness is of utmost importance. Only recently has the world become aware of Colombia's positive traits such as the abundant natural resources and varied climates. Located on the north-western corner of the continent next to the Panama Canal, Colombia is the gateway to South America with coastlines on both the Atlantic and the Pacific Oceans. Three branches of the Andes mountain range traverse the country from South to North. Beautiful valleys, generously bathed by rivers and lakes, enrich the land and make it fertile for a great variety of tropical fruit, flowers and other produce. The land is green and rich, and there are large areas covered with dense forests.

Aside from these blessings, Colombia's mines are famous for yielding the finest emeralds in the world. Gold, coal, silver, platinum and salt mines are among it´s underground treasures. Coal is Colombia's most important source of income, followed by coffee, bananas and cut flowers.

For over three decades, Colombia has been the second largest exporter of cut flowers in the world. Holland, as always, ranks number one. When flying towards Bogotá, the first thing you see as you approach the city are the greenhouses where flowers grow by the millions. Roses, pompons, carnations, orchids, callas, exotics and other varieties are exported worldwide all year 'round. The beneficial growing conditions and the expertise of those who bring their perishable products to foreign markets make this possible. Even though the U.S. dollar has fallen in relation to the Colombian peso over the last two years, affecting the growers' income, Colombia is still the second exporter of fresh flowers in the world.

Colombian coffee has been famous for its quality and mild flavour for many decades. Juan Valdéz, with his hat and moustache, riding his mule Conchita that carries eternal sacks of coffee saddled on each side, will long be remembered around the world.

Our wildlife is rich and varied. Birds and jungle animals have been exported to zoos all over the world. It's a shame their origins are usually labelled with a generic 'From South America'. Also, the tropical location allows a great variety of fruits to be harvested; some crops can be harvested three times a year. Hopefully, when security improves and landowners can return to their farms, the export of tropical fruit will flourish again.

Aside from the more common fruits, Colombian farmers grow exotic varieties such as curuba, lulo, maracuyá, guanábana, uchuva, chirimoya, pitaya, feijoa, granadilla, and many more. There is no translation for these fruits that are unknown in most parts of the world.

Anyone who has tasted a 'sorbete de curuba' (curuba smoothie) or a 'sorbete de lulo', made with fruit pulp, milk and sugar, will long remember the unique flavor. A 'sorbete de guanábana' needs a few teaspoons of lemon juice and a little 'aguardiente' (anise brandy). Another tasty fruit called feijoa is known to have aphrodisiac properties. And, no one could forget the marvelous taste of a pitaya, ideal for relieving a stopped up stomach.

Every area of Colombia holds its own distinctive charm. The fusion of races, music, rituals, history, food, traditions, coastlines, vegetation and natural splendor will hopefully, once again, make Colombia one of the most fascinating and visited tourist sites in Latin America.

Sad to say, because there is so much valuable, raw material in the land and mines, both Colombians and foreign 'gold prospectors' have been corrupted by the get-rich-easy syndrome and much of the land has been ruined by illicit mining and harvesting prime material for narcotics.

Chapter 28

MY TREASURES

ONE AFTERNOON, WHILE we were walking down the mountain for daily exercise, I found a four-leaf clover. Hey, that's good luck! Soon, all of us, even Sandra, began to search for more. I had a hard time searching without my eyeglasses that had been 'lost' along with my purse and all its contents on the day of my abduction. Nevertheless, a few more four-leaf clovers came my way and I decided to dry them for mementos that I would give to special friends when I went free.

I showed Sandra how to dry her clovers in her notebook but my friendliness didn´t soften her up one bit. She refused to let me have two sheets of paper so I pressed mine between two flat stones inside my tent, letting them dry for ten days. They turned out quite well.

Ever since Alacrán seized my bigger blanket I was so cold at night I could hardly sleep. How I longed for the warmth of a sleeping bag! I decided to make one out of my small blanket. By chance, there was some string in my plastic bag and it occurred to me that I could make a needle out of a small, wooden stick. I used another little stick to pierce two holes in my blanket before each stitch, protecting my make-shift 'needle' from breaking. It took many 'needles' to sew the blanket at one end and up one side, but it was well worth my trouble. That night I slept like a baby. I made a sleeping bag for Carlos the next day and was soon awarded the title of 'official sleeping-bag manufacturer'.

I wore the same clothes day and night during the whole ordeal, rotating the inner layers (inside-out) every day and washing twice a week.

One day, when Victor was in a good mood, he came up with a joke: "The comandante tells his group of hostages, 'Guys, I have great news for you! Tomorrow you'll get to change your underwear!' Everybody was very excited, Hurray, hurray!' Then he added, "I command each of you to exchange your underwear at once . . . with the person standing at your right."

Leaving the tent to urinate three or four times every night, especially when it was raining, was very uncomfortable. I found a big plastic bottle and asked William to cut off its upper third to make a 'chamber pot'. It was such a relief not to go out in the rain! Washing my cherished, new toilet early every morning became my first chore.

On one unusually sunny day I needed a hat to protect my face. Rummaging through my plastic 'bag of treasures' in search of something to use, I found a little, cardboard Colgate box, perfect for a visor, and an empty, woven plastic sack. I asked William to cut me a square piece (we didn´t have access to cutting devices) that would cover my head and two long pieces to make strings for my 'bonnet'. I asked him to cut part of the Colgate box into the shape of a visor for my 'bonnet'. I sewed the pieces together to form a strange-looking, but efficient hat. At last my face was protected from the burning sun . . . when it wasn´t raining.

We all had a hearty laugh when my friends saw me wearing my new creation. Manuel suggested that as soon as I returned to Bogotá, I should take it to the Colgate-Palmolive people as a publicity item. "Maybe they'll even pay your ransom," he joked. Federico said my hat was too ugly to wear, but I didn't care. After all, there was nobody I wanted to seduce or be romantic with, and anything that protected my face from burning was fine with me. Any vanity I held on to was long gone after being without a comb, brush or mirror for several months.

We enjoyed these few moments of amusement, but there was always an underlying sadness and uncertainty that brought thoughts to our minds we had never considered before.

In my 'bag of treasures' I kept a tiny piece of broken mirror that Blanca had left behind. I kept it so I would have something to cut my veins if I became very ill and decided I couldn't stand it any longer. What was Blanca's reason for keeping it? She never told me, but I am sure it was similar to mine. When I told Victor and Manuel about my broken mirror, they assured me it wasn't unusual for people in our circumstances to have suicidal thoughts.

Chapter 29

MORE NEWCOMERS

THE ARRIVAL OF a new prisoner interrupted the monotony of one of those gray mornings. His name was **Augusto**. He was a good looking young man in his late thirties. Three nights earlier on his way home from the gym, they caught him in the same way most of us had been captured. He was the Sales Manager of a cattle ranch belonging to a family that had to leave the country for security reasons. The FARC mistook him for one of the owners and sent a group of criminals to take him.

Augusto was sceptical about the company paying his ransom. One of their executives had been kidnapped the year before and to avoid becoming an on-going target for FARC extortions, the Board of Directors decided to change the office's phone numbers whenever one of their employees was abducted.

After the first night, Augusto complained that the freezing wind blowing through his tent kept him awake all night. I asked him to give me his blanket and made him a sleeping bag. Augusto was very grateful and became a true friend. He stood by me when I needed encouragement, a shoulder to cry on, or any other support. The next day Augusto saw me fall in the mud on my way to the 'chonto'. He worked hard all day, searching for flat stones that he placed carefully along the path to make our trips to the 'chonto' easier.

Augusto had a beautiful smile, a sparkling personality, and an amazing capacity to adapt to anything. When the thugs forced him out of his car, he managed to sneak along a small overnight case and a down feathered jacket. It was delightful to clip my nails with a real nail-clipper! Most of the time, Augusto was positive and encouraging, but as time went by, we would sometimes cry together when we talked about our children and my grandchildren.

Now, there were four thoughtful and attentive young men in our group. When I told them how much I appreciated their kindness and how they reminded me of my sons, they told me I reminded them of their mothers and how difficult it would be to see them live through a situation like mine.

As I was climbing out of my tent one morning, Federico told me three new hostages had been brought in at daybreak.

Mauricio, 75 years old, was a heavy-set, retired lawyer. He had been captured eight days earlier at his home in Anapoima. Mauricio was exhausted. They had forced him to walk for five days along the cliffs of the Andes, spending the nights in the open air. It relieved him to know he would no longer be alone in the company of his sinister escorts. He and his wife had planned to retire at their small country house. Unfortunately, after forty years of a happy, childless marriage, his wife died in a car accident.

The other two new captives were **Franco and Teresa**. Franco owned a bakery in Anapoima. He was a short man of about 60 with gray-hair. Teresa, his girlfriend, who also managed his bakery, was an attractive woman in her late thirties. The bandits intercepted Franco's car when he was driving Teresa home, where she lived with her mother and her eight-year old son.

Teresa had fallen off the horse and sprained her ankle. She was in great pain and severely bruised. Like every newcomer, she was depressed and cried all the time. Claudio announced that since Teresa was only an employee, she would be sent home in a few days.

Victor and Federico helped Franco set up their tent on the only rather dry spot available close to the 'rancha' (eating place). The next morning they complained that their tent was full of smoke. Manuel helped Franco set it up again with the opening facing in the opposite direction. The smoke problem was solved but that didn´t take away the sadness and the cold.

Claudio gave every newcomer a camouflaged uniform, a jacket and a pair of boots. Alacrán took blankets from Victor and Federico, giving one to Mauricio and Augusto, and the other to Teresa and Franco. Still, Teresa complained about the cold but Claudio refused to provide them with another blanket.

A few days later, two 'guerrilleros' who knew Teresa from her home town, were sent to persuade her to join the FARC on a permanent basis. She wisely replied, "I am honored by the invitation but my mother and son need me."

There weren't enough pots and spoons to go around so I shared mine with Franco and Teresa. Franco had a pocket-knife and dug fifteen holes into the cover of my little eating pot that made a solitaire game in the shape of a triangle, similar to Chinese checkers. I scavenged some beans where the food was stored to use instead of marbles

After playing, I left my solitaire and beans in a little box in my tent, next to my imaginary pillow. That night, I suddenly woke up to the grisly sensation of an animal crawling on me. By instinct, I covered my face with my arm while the animal slithered over me to get to the beans. I had no intention of fighting an animal in the darkness, so I patiently listened to the thing devouring the beans. After having his midnight snack, the critter slipped away.

The next day, while hunting for something to keep my new set of beans covered, I found an excellent solution—a small can with a lid. By the way, only once did we get beans for a meal, and they were as hard as bullets. When I suggested to William they might let them soak in water overnight, he gave me his big, monkey-like smile. We never had beans again.

Chapter 30

DISCRIMINATION

RAFAEL CAME TO my tent and began his usual blah-blah-blah about not needing Viagra and fantasizing about "our trip to the United States together." This fellow was truly nothing but a pain in the ass. Unfortunately, there was nowhere I could go to avoid his presence, so I simply ignored his comments and only gave him friendly advice: "Go back to your family as soon as you are free."

Estela didn't agree with me. "Rafael is a prince—you shouldn't miss this opportunity to find real love. You two could make a lovely couple, let him warm your feet when you're cold." Estela couldn't understand that I didn't like Rafael in the least and would never settle for a relationship with him.

"I wouldn't be interested in Rafael if he was the last Coca-Cola in the desert," I told her. Eventually, Rafael got the point that I wasn't going to give in, and became very aggressive towards me. He gave me a nick-name, "Myriam, Queen of the Latrine." I didn't say anything out loud, but of course I didn't like it—especially when I heard Faber, the 'guerrillero', repeat it. I told Rafael to please leave me alone. To my relief, this kept the man at a distance.

Nevertheless, he must have told Franco and Teresa something to turn them against me. Their friendly attitude changed abruptly.

Teresa told me, "Aside from our age difference, we come from different cultures." Under normal circumstances, it wouldn't have bothered me to be rejected. But we depended on each other's fellowship and support, and it hurt to be discriminated by a few of my companions. My friendship with Victor, Federico, Manuel and Augusto never changed—but it must have affected me because I stopped writing my 'coplas'.

Chapter 31

GRASPING FOR HOPE

As TIME WENT by, our hopes faded. It was a test of patience just to wait, without news or evidence that something was working in our favor. Late in the afternoons, when it started to get dark and we stood in a circle holding hands, praying, we looked up into the sky to watch the formation of the clouds. Sometimes they took on different shapes and figures which we liked to believe were omens of the future. One evening we saw a vertical cloud which distinctly resembled the image of a Madonna.

Victor said, "This means someone in our group will be liberated very soon." It didn't happen.

Whenever there was a clear, starry night and a full moon we knew the tents would be covered with a heavy crust of ice the next morning. On these mornings, I stayed in my tent and didn't go out for breakfast.

Sweet memories kept my spirit up and warmed my heart on the cold nights when I shivered in my tent. I would close my eyes and search in my mind to bring back my favorite moments. Once, I traveled back to a warm night at 'Buganviles'. We had turned out the lights on the terrace to watch thousands of tiny, blinking fireflies. Oh, how I missed those evenings with my family!

David and I often played our accordions and the dogs, "Sacha", "Pochi" and "Pitufo" always joined in, howling and 'singing' to our music. What a choir!

On cooler evenings we stayed in the house, barbequed some meat in the fireplace and drank a few cups of wine. When we were ready to go to bed, we ordered the dogs to go outside. Sacha, our enormous Great Dane, would carefully squeeze her head under the coffee table and stay very quiet. She must have believed she was 'perfectly hidden' and had us fooled.

A little sparrow woke me up every morning at exactly six a.m., tapping on my window. An hour later, a group of about fifty green parakeets flew over Buganviles, squawking exactly like a pack of barking dogs. The parakeets caused uproar among the dogs in the neighbourhood and together, they all formed the daily, daybreak concert.

And there was "Sir Peacock", who strutted proudly up and down the driveway, constantly admiring himself in my shiny, old car's bumpers. It is during these difficult times that one realizes how seemingly, trivial moments are so much more meaningful than important accomplishments.

Chapter 32

CARLOS AND PEDRO
ARE RELEASED

AFTER THREE MONTHS of captivity, when our captors finally realized there wasn't anybody in his family who could pay his ransom, Carlos, the owner of the duffle-bag stand, was released. He was quite a remarkable person and I respected him as a loyal friend.

He was born into a very poor family where the father drank away every peso he earned and constantly mistreated his wife. She ended up abandoning him and her other four children, taking the baby with her. This left Carlos, the oldest boy, 'responsible' for his two older sisters and his younger brother.

At that time it wasn't mandatory for all children in Colombia to attend school. From the time he was ten, Carlos had to work hard to support his siblings. He milked cows, carried heavy sacks at the market-place and ran errands. They lived with one of their aunts for the first two years after their mother's departure. After that, these poor children were passed around from one relative to another. Some of us cried when Carlos told us about his childhood. Nevertheless, his sad upbringing strengthened him. He became a self-made man. He managed to educate himself and was knowledgeable in world history and international affairs.

When he was twenty and had a job, he tried to reunite what was left of his family. He located his mother and then his father, hoping they could live together and make up for lost time. But Carlos' dream didn't work out as he hoped. His father was still drinking and actively cooperating with the FARC, who were growing fast in the region. However, four decades later, his father's link to the bandits turned out to be a favorable factor for Carlos' final release.

Early one morning, 'guerilleros' from another camp came to pick up Carlos. These two were assigned to escort the captives to a place of release. I didn't dare give him a note for my family because three of the bandits were standing around his tent. All I could do was to wish him luck and ask him to leave me his tooth-brush. It was new when he got it, and he was the only one to use it over those three months. From that day on, I used my old toothbrush to brush the mud off the outer layer of my clothing. I had two good reasons to be thankful that day. One was Carlos´ release, and the other was to have a fairly decent toothbrush.

As was our custom when someone was released, we honored Carlos that evening in our prayers. We didn't know it, but because there wasn't any money in sight for the FARC, he was sent out on his own to find his way across the mountain range.

We all discussed leaving the country with our families and staying away until Colombia recovered its security and peace. Most of us had relatives living in other countries, mainly the United States, Canada, and Spain.

Federico said, "Since we have so much free time, why don't we practice our English for an hour every day?" Pedro added, "Myriam, could you give me a few lessons? I'm planning to go and live with my daughter in Chicago as soon as this ordeal is over with." Of course I obliged, it was a nice way to pass the time.

Pedro, who had been Carlos' tent-mate, was depressed and acting strangely. Like many other kidnapped people, he vacillated between believing his family was making every effort to liberate him, and doubting if they were at all interested in seeing him again. When he was fortunate enough to be sent home, I asked him to deliver another note to my family, which read:

"My beloved Sons, don't worry, I'm OK. I'm sure you sent my medicine but it didn't reach me. Please try again. I have faith in God that you are negotiating successfully. Paying ransom is my only possibility to freedom. I love you and miss you so much. 1000 hugs and kisses from your Omi".

After Pedro left, Claudio went into his tent and found six new sets of men's underwear, six new T-shirts, three flashlights, four new batteries and many plastic bags. It seemed strange that Pedro was hiding these things knowing how much his companions needed them—Augusto and Manuel didn't even have a second pair of shorts. Federico told me that he noticed a drastic change in Pedro's attitude after Simón forced him to dig his own grave.

I inherited a T-shirt and a comb from Pedro. After three months, I finally had a comb! I asked Sandra to let me take a look in her mirror. Oh, what a shock!!! About three inches of white roots had grown out on each side of my head and messy, faded-brown, dyed hair hung down on each side of my sad-looking face. I was used to having my hair done every week, and the roots dyed every month. It was truly better not to have a mirror under these circumstances; this was the first time I had ever seen myself with white eyebrows, and the effect was catastrophic. I looked ancient.

I looked like an old, drug-addict street bum! In Colombia, these people are labelled with a cruel title: 'desechables', which means 'disposables'. My complexion was a disaster—my face was deeply burned, and I had scabs on my forehead and dark spots all over my face and hands. Also, due to my fast weight loss—forty-six pounds—my face was so wrinkled I looked about thirty years older.

Now, my wardrobe consisted of three T-shirts, one sweatshirt, one FARC uniform, my red 'jacket', two sweat-pants, my smelly rubber boots, my lovely Colgate bonnet, and a blanket over my shoulders. I always held my trusty walking stick by my side. The mirror episode only aggravated my depression when I realized I looked even worse than I had imagined.

In an attempt to cheer me up, Federico said, "Soon, we will all return home to our loving families and everything we have been through will be forgotten. Myriam, an entirely new life is coming your way; be happy and look forward to it. Don't stay in Bogotá. You should live somewhere close to your son in the United States."

Manuel offered to cut my hair and this became the event of the month! Everyone stood around to watch. The haircut didn't do much to help my appearance, but I knew my looks were the least of my worries; most of my efforts were geared on survival. I taught myself to be grateful for not being sicker than I was and still able to laugh at myself. I composed a new copla:

"Ese look desechable
que'adquirió l'abuelita,
trapo, botas y bastón
y ahora su gorrita"

"With her street-bum look
Ole Gramma's looking fine

Rags, walk'n stick'n boots
with'er bonnet,she's divine."

Meanwhile In Bogotá:

Charlie kept calling every week and David always gave him a new reason to lower the ransom to a sum he and his brothers could pay. His tactic was to always let Charlie set the tone, and keep with it. Sometimes they communicated in a rather friendly way, but when Charlie was mean, David was even meaner. Nevertheless, at the end, he always made it clear that the family was most willing to cooperate, but the amount they were demanding was still completely out of their reach. Suddenly, David had to travel to the U.S. for an emergency. For two weeks he was replaced by someone else in the 'Comité' who followed David's 'diplomatic' tactics.

Chapter 33

VISITING WITH THE GUERRILLEROS

A FEW TIMES William and Sandra came to my tent to chat and smoke a cigarette. Once I asked William what his favorite music was. His smart reply was: "Fundamentalmente, casettes" (Fundamentally, cassettes). Ma fam'ly owns a yucca plantation and I used ta make two million pesos a month (roughly $700 U.S.) growin' yuccas. I neva got home til'I spent ma last peso at a whore house."

Two million pesos is a good amount of money for a Colombian peasant family with three small children. When I asked him what his reason was for joining the FARC, he said, "It's a lot of fun! We party like crazy when we kill a bunch of 'vultures', (meaning soldiers) or shit-up a town".

When I asked William what was so great about attacking a town full of helpless people, and leaving them without a home, his only reply was a big, monkey-like smile. Still, to me, he was the less uncouth of the whole bunch.

Claudio was the best-looking person in the camp and he knew it. He was very conceited. When he sensed someone watching him, he would show off by chopping wood with one hand.

His tent was on a higher level, facing ours so he could keep a close watch on us. Sometimes he would call out when a group of guerrilla girls were passing by and invite them for a visit. Unless they were on an emergency mission, they usually took him up on his offer. During his bouts of hospitality, Claudio made sure everybody knew what was going on. There was no discretion and they didn't even bother to take their boots off. The rubber footwear sticking out of the door of the tent made those episodes even more amusing, and the provocative noises left little to one´s imagination.

* * * * * *

One day, foul mouthed Raquel was on duty to watch us at the 'chonto'. She had insulted us furiously the previous evening. My curiosity got the better of me and I asked her, "Raquel, why do you hate us so much"? She answered, "Cos ya'r all just a bunch o'rich #%$&%)sons o'bitches."

"What do you mean by rich?" I asked. "Ya'eat breakfast when ya git up every day, don'tcha?" she retorted.

* * * * * *

My body was craving protein. One day our captors were eating a pile of trout they caught in the river. Claudio noticed my hungry look as I watched them.

"If ya want, someday I'll catch ya a trout".

"That would be so nice of you, Comandante—but it wouldn't be fair to my companions, and I wouldn't enjoy being the only captive to eat a delicious trout. We would appreciate it if you could catch one for each of us." Of course, this never happened.

*   *   *   *   *   *

One day Sandra brought a little rabbit to the camp. It was wonderful to have a pet to cuddle. I loved it from the moment I saw it, and the little thing also took a liking to me. Sandra tied him up but he always managed to escape for a visit. This adventurous little rabbit had to travel a distance of about five blocks, cross a stream and pass all the tents to find its way to mine and curl up on my lap.

About a week later, when I returned to my tent after bathing at "Mathusaleah's pond", I found the little rabbit's fur outside my tent. Faber had slaughtered it for some unknown reason. It couldn't have served him for a meal since it was only fur and bones. Did it bother him that the rabbit was disobedient to the FARC's high command and ran away to visit me?

*   *   *   *   *   *

Franco taught us a card game called 'Molestando al Vecino', (Annoying your Neighbor) which could be played by six to eight people. There was only one less muddy spot nearby, about fifteen square feet. It was on higher ground, away from the marshy area where everything else took place. Augusto and Manuel dragged two heavy logs and set them facing each other. We placed a black plastic bag in the middle to use as a 'table'. Augusto's pink marker came in handy to color over the almost invisible hearts and diamonds on the old cards. I hoped that someday we would be in the right mood to play charades.

Shortly after we arranged our little gathering place, Claudio ordered Alacrán and Raquel to destroy it. They turned it into a mini-tejo court for their recreation. Again, we resorted to playing cards in my tent where only five people could sit at one time. Whenever it was raining, everybody's boots were brought inside. Pee-uuu, what a smell!!!

*   *   *   *   *   *

'Tejo' is a traditional game played by peasant men in Colombia. Two boxes filled with clay and a bit of gunpowder (the target) are placed at opposite ends of a rather long and narrow court. With a bottle of beer in one hand each player takes turns throwing the 'tejo', a flat stone slab, at the opposite target. There wasn't enough dry land available to do it properly, so Claudio had to settle for a 'Mini-tejo' court. They used coins for 'tejos' and instead of gun powder they made a mark at the center of the clay. Of course there was no beer.

Some of us were watching Victor, Rafael and Manuel play 'tejo' with the 'guerrilleros'. Suddenly, Rafael's face turned very pale and he desperately grabbed for Claudio's hand. Claudio roughly pulled his hand away and yelled, "Now, are ya gonna play, or are ya gonna die"?

Rafael had another epileptic seizure and fell in the sludge. Victor quickly ran to Sandra's tent in search of something to inject.

In very calm manner Sandra said, "I threw all ma medicine in the river when we moved last time. Ya think I´s gonna carry all that garbage around?" Consequently, there wasn't even one aspirin available in the camp. The Compañía, the only resource for any kind of assistance, had recently moved far away from the other camps so there was no way to help Rafael.

Victor was so frustrated, he cried. All he could do was place a piece of wood between Rafael's teeth to protect him from swallowing his tongue. Manuel helped Victor carry Rafael to his tent. Despite my feelings towards him, it saddened me to see Rafael have a seizure in these deplorable conditions.

Claudio and Faber immediately ran to drain the water out of one of the coffin-shaped trenches. They must have been sure he was dying and needed an empty hole to get his body out of the way. We prayed for Rafael and for the medicine that he and all of us needed so desperately to reach us.

On the other hand, we did have proof that God was listening to our prayers. Considering our situation, we all remained fairly healthy. It was a miracle no one got pneumonia or any of the infectious illnesses that often afflicted our captors. We were much older, but other than Rafael's epileptic seizures and everybody's bruises and depressions, we were surviving.

The next day Rafael was back on his feet. With the mirror and brush he had claimed from Pedro, and his usual air of importance, he spent hours every day admiring himself while he combed his beard, seated on his throne (an empty plastic five-gallon can) which was our best and only piece of furniture.

Our captors told him that when the FARC called his home to demand the ransom, the young woman he lived with, answered, "I don't have a cent so you might as well keep that son-of-a-bitch".

A few days later they asked Rafael if there was someone else in his family they should contact. He gave them his son and ex-wife's numbers. They must have had the right connections, and Rafael was released within a few days. Three months seems like an eternity for a kidnapped person. Nevertheless, it was a short time compared to most other cases. When he left, Rafael took the only hair-brush and mirror in the camp. He explained, "I must look my best to meet the press at my arrival."

Looking back, I realize that this man´s annoying attitudes were only symptoms that he was rapidly 'going off his rocker'. It took me time to understand this because I was also in an emotionally delicate state.

Chapter 34

TORTUOUS ACTIONS

I WAS DEEPLY affected by an exceptionally brutal act. One afternoon, when passing by Alacrán's tent, I stopped to hear the news on his radio. The FARC had invaded the home of a humble family in a town called Chiquinquirá. A woman was forced to kneel, while they locked a 'collar' made of styro-foam tubes around her neck, in the presence of her husband and their four children. The tubes were stuffed with explosives and the device had a remote control. The husband was told that the collar would only be removed when their family paid the FARC the amount of fifteen million pesos (U.S $5.000).

The macabre collar was programmed to explode at 6 p.m., exactly nine hours after it was set in place around this poor woman's neck. During those hours, two policemen from the Anti-explosive Unit tried desperately to deactivate it. Fifteen million pesos is a lot of money in a small town, even for someone who owns a prosperous business. The majority of the common people in Colombia could never have access to this sum, much less at short notice.

That evening we took turns standing outside Alacrán's tent to listen to his radio. The report said that despite the officers´ efforts, they hadn't been able to deactivate the bomb. Of course none of us could sleep when we got back to our tents. The incident reminded us once again that our lives were in the hands of psychopaths who were capable of carrying out such unscrupulous, diabolical plans.

The next morning, we heard the report that the device on the woman's neck had exploded, killing her and one of the policemen. The other officer lost his right hand. We were all heart-broken. At breakfast, I noticed that some of the bandits couldn't wipe the smirk off their faces. I asked Faber what his good mood was all about, "That #%$@^&* old hag got what she deserved", was his answer. There was so much hatred in that boy's face.

Two years after the gruesome crime had taken place, the FARC denied publically that they had anything to do with it.

*   *   *   *   *   *

A woman I knew as a girl from school many years ago was kidnapped two years before me. She was rebellious and refused to eat. Even though her family paid the agreed ransom, she died in captivity and her body was not even sent to her family for a humane burial.

And the long list of unjust and cruel acts carried out by the terrorists, goes on. One of the most difficult factors to deal with was the knowledge of their capacity to hate and kill.

Chapter 35

GAS CYLINDERS

Sometimes, while looking up at the gray, arid mountain range around us, we would see long lines of mules carrying small gas cylinders towards the Compañía. They reminded me of a TV program I saw in Bogotá shortly before my abduction. The news channel broadcasted a video that had been seized by the Colombian Army, demonstrating the FARC's training methods for newly enlisted guerrillas. It clearly explained, in minute detail, their bomb making techniques and strategies to blow up small towns. The small gas cylinders were stuffed with dynamite, mixed with broken glass and scraps of metal, previously soaked in acid. Then it showed the resulting destruction, the terrorists counting the money they stole from the town's bank, the booty obtained from other lootings, and the wild celebration that followed.

After destroying the police station and killing the four or five policemen on guard, the terrorists proceeded to explode more bombs, indiscriminately, in the most populated areas. When the townspeople saw hundreds of 'guerrilleros' walking toward their town, they knew what awaited them. All they could do was find a place to hide.

Amid the rubble and ruins of their humble homes, their children's schools and their primitive medical facilities, the survivors were left with nothing but the clothes on their backs. They were usually too shocked to fight back and wouldn't dare to express their hatred of the FARC terrorists. Meanwhile, the 'victorious' forces raised their revolutionary flags under the pretence of rescuing their fellow countrymen from poverty and government abandonment. Then, before the Army had time to arrive, the attackers fled rapidly to the refuge of their 'safe haven'.

Statistics from El Tiempo, Colombia's main newspaper, dated September 13, 2001, revealed that in the three previous years, the guerrillas had attacked 161 towns in this manner. They reported sixty abandoned 'ghost towns' throughout the country. The numbers of these towns kept on growing. Not a living soul stayed behind where there had been so much bloodshed and death. Weeds grew up between the cracks in the ruins of the houses—crops and animals had long since died. Nothing but desolation remained.

Another criminal practice of the FARC against the innocent population, is still the use of 'minas quiebra-patas' (landmines). They carefully bury small amounts of explosives in the ground, usually close to schools and other gathering places. Anyone who accidentally steps on one of these landmines ends up dead, blind, or seriously wounded. There are hundreds of mutilated people all over the country; victims of these landmines. Only the sick and wicked minds of FARC leaders could possibly carry out such devilish actions.

Chapter 36

DESPLAZADOS (THE HOMELESS)

DURING THE WORST years of the conflict, every day approximately two hundred people left everything behind in their towns or little farms in search of safety, thereby enlarging the slums of 'desplazados'. Belts of extreme poverty grew on the outskirts of most big cities throughout Colombia. Poor families, usually with three or more children, fled from their homes, suffering a hopeless destiny.

They invaded the stoplights and main roads to collect a few coins for survival. Some offer to clean windshields, others perform feats such as living statues or fire-eating. And others sell flowers, fruit, water, sodas, books, toys and various other items on the streets. The children do acrobatic skills, while their mothers carry signs begging for a few coins to buy food.

The government entity called "Red de Solidaridad" (Solidarity Network) in charge of these families, is doing as much as they can. Regrettably, this entity does not have enough funds or workers to get directly involved.

Cazucá, the main displaced neighbourhood on the outskirts of Bogota, is a squalid collection of tin shacks where hundreds of families are sheltered under blue plastic sheets. Their main concern is bare survival. A few years ago, there were only three hoses to provide water to the entire area.

These people have lost their culture, their social standing, and everything they ever worked for and accomplished. This disastrous situation is causing a tremendous rift in the fabric of the underprivileged Colombian society.

Shortly after I returned to freedom I met Barbara, a good-looking, young, black woman who was selling flowers at a traffic light. She came from Chocó, Colombia's poorest State, located on the Pacific coast and western border of Colombia. Her boy was four and her baby girl was one year old when they arrived in Bogotá eight months earlier. She had to flee from her home town when the FARC murdered her husband and twelve other people. When attempting to escape, a 'guerrillero' slashed her elbow with a 'machete'.

The first month Barbara and her babies slept on the street. Then they were received into a shelter under a plastic roof. Sometimes the Red Cross provided food for them, but finding work was almost impossible for someone in her situation.

I also met a peasant woman in her fifties. Fanny, her husband and their fifteen and seventeen year old sons fled from their farm in the Eastern Plains to save the boys from being forcibly recruited by the FARC.

"We had to leave everything we owned and travel to Bogotá in search of work and a safer life. We only took the title deeds to our small farm, a backpack with a few clothes, and a birdcage with our three parrots, which we sold to pay for our bus fares," Fanny told me.

Their troubles began when a group of heavily armed FARC subversives entered their farm to enlist her sons. When Fanny told them that her boys were studying in the nearby town, she was warned, "Ya think we givá shit'bout that? If the guys don't enlist, ya better be out'a here by eight o'clock tamorrow morning, or the whole family's dead!"

Fanny knew this was a serious threat. Only a few days earlier she saw them cut off a neighbour's penis and leave him on a road, bleeding to death, in the presence of his family. They had protested when the FARC came to enlist their boys. After that, they tied one of their sons to a car and pulled him along the stone road until his body was torn to pieces and he died. Fanny cried when she remembered the horrendous scenes.

The widow and her other son currently dwell in one of Bogotá's slums, trying to adapt to their loneliness. They suffer from cold and poverty they had never experienced before. Her son found a job in a car repair shop, and she works as a house cleaner for one of my friends. In spite of their desperate situation, they consider themselves lucky to earn enough money for food and to have a roof over their heads.

After my release, I went to an open air event that took place in a park next to the slums where many 'desplazados' live. Approximately ten organizations came together to hand out Christmas presents to over six-thousand children. These toys had been confiscated by customs when they were being smuggled into the country. How overwhelming it was to be in direct contact with hundreds of displaced families and see, first hand, the tragedy and hopelessness in their eyes! Children interviewed on TV agreed that this was their only happy day since they left their homes. It was sad to hear a little girl say she missed her cow, her chicken, and her daily egg.

*   *   *   *   *   *

One of the most devastating incidents in Colombia's desolate areas took place on April 2002, in the town of Bojayá, Chocó. The FARC and the Paramilitaries were fighting for control over the coca plantations in the area. There was no Army or Police nearby, and the shooting drove the town population to seek refuge in the local church. The FARC thugs threw a gas cylinder bomb into the church and it exploded. One hundred and nineteen people died that day, hundreds were wounded, and forty were missing. Most of the victims were children. The bridge connecting Bojayá with the rest of the country was also blown up. The presence of terrorist groups delayed air transport for the wounded and medical help for the rest of the town's people.

Chapter 37

PANCHITA

LATE ONE AFTERNOON, while praying, we saw two young fellows approach the camp dragging a tiny, old woman towards us. They dropped her at our feet the way a dog drops his prey when he brings it to the hunter.

Her light summer clothing was filthy and soaking wet, and so were her once-white sandals. The bandits had no consideration for the fact that this poor woman could have been about one hundred years old. 'Panchita's feet were numb from the cold and she was suffering from dehydration. She was shivering uncontrollably and babbled words that didn't make sense.

There was still a small fire left in the 'rancha' from the last meal. William filled the big pot with water from the well, heated it to bath temperature, and with Augusto's help, carried it to a spot close to my tent. After washing Panchita, I dressed her in whatever I could gather from our group. The warm water comforted her, and after she drank some hot 'aguapanela' and took an aspirin she asked me, "Where am I, su mercé?" I didn't want to upset her so I told her to try to get some sleep—we would have lots of time to chat in the morning.

'Panchita' and I slept in my 'bed'. I wanted to care of her like Blanca had cared for me the evening of my arrival. The next day 'Panchita' remembered some of the last days' happenings, "They were awaiting for me when I got off the bus. They followed me into the house. I have a bump on my head because the man who forced me to drink something from a bottle hit me when I refused." She had been captured at her home in the same area as most of us.

She told me, "I live in Bogotá with one of my daughters and visit my 'viejito' (little old man) every week in Anapoima. He has a disease with a foreign name and doesn't remember anything."

It was hard to believe that this tiny person had six daughters, a son, twenty-two grandchildren, and four great-grandchildren. Soon I learned how bright and spunky she was. She had been doing yoga for the last fifteen years. A few days later, when she felt well enough, she encouraged some of us to join her in her morning workouts. It wasn't easy to keep up with little Panchita.

She was amazing! She adapted to her new situation faster than anyone else, and gained everyone's affection from the very first moment. Even some of the 'guerrilleros' were a bit less hostile to her than to the rest of us. When we went to our bathing spot, I noticed that the icy water didn't bother her at all. She kneeled down to scrub her clothes on a stone as if she'd always done it that way.

"I was born a country girl and I´m used to a tough life," she said. "You know those bandits stole the money I had in my purse. What can I do to hide my ring and bracelet?"

"We'll ask Estela to lend us a needle and thread so that we can sew your valuables inside your shirt pocket to keep them out of sight. But you must remember never to hang your shirt out to dry!" I told her.

My experience in the unspoken ways of the camp came in handy. I passed on the advice Manuel gave me when I arrived, "If a 'guerrillero' visits you in your tent and, in an overly-affectionate manner asks you something like, "Since 'su mercé' will be released soon, would you please leave me your watch to remember you by?" You can say: "Do I have to?"

His answer will probably be, "Oh, no, but I am sure you want to leave me a memento since we've been such good friends." Then you can be a hypocrite just like he is and say something these ignorant people can understand, "I would love to, because you are so dear to me—but unfortunately I can't. My husband would kill me if I dare to return without his special gift."

'Su mercé' is an old, respectful term, used by servants when they speak to their 'patrón'. Simple people use it as an affectionate way to address someone. Manuel's advice came in handy when Raquel approached me and tried her 'su mercé' on me hoping I would give her my watch. It didn't work.

A week later, 'Claudio' called 'Panchita', "Hey Abuela (Grandma). Got somethin' for ya". He gave her a bag her daughters had sent containing medicine, a pair of tiny rubber boots, a sweat-suit, two sweaters, two warm pajamas, a wool blanket, wool socks, Pond's cream, shampoo, etc. This changed 'Panchita's life. She returned my socks and t-shirt and gave me a little jar of Ponds cream—a delightful change from the cooking oil.

Suspecting she must have had some good contacts, I told her Carlos had been released when they confirmed that his father had maintained a friendly relationship with the FARC many years before. She remembered that her brother and 'Tirofijo' (the FARC top dog) were friends in their childhood years. She said her brother donated a farm to the FARC when he became rich. Even though she told this to Claudio, they made no exception for her. The FARC kept her just as long as any other kidnapped person, until her family paid the ransom.

Chapter 38

A NEEDLE AND A KNIGHT

A Needle In A Hay Stack

Some of my friends were uncomfortable because their clothes were coming apart. I told them I would be glad to mend them if we could find some thread and a needle. Sandra lent me the one and only needle and thread available. Unluckily, I dropped it in the straw while trying to thread it and found myself literally, "searching for a needle in a haystack." I was scared. I wondered what my punishment would be if I couldn't return such a valuable object. Would they chain me to a pole, or maybe chain my foot to someone else's, as they sometimes do? I asked God for His help, just as I do every time I'm in trouble. In my desperate search, I soon found the needle!

*   *   *   *   *   *

THE KNIGHT IN RUSTY ARMOUR

One day Manuel came to my tent and brought me a book entitled, *The Knight in Rusty Armor by Robert Fisher,* which he found in the mud. There was nothing else available for us to read, aside from some FARC communist flyers. After he read it, he passed it around.

It was a beautiful, meaningful story that must have been sent to us by God. My tent was unusually bright on that sunny day and I was able to read it without my glasses. I had never seen a book with such large print.

The story was about a knight who believed he was perfect in every way: caring, generous and amorous. He never took off his armor so he would always be ready to save every young woman in distress from evil . . . even when the lady didn't want to be saved.

Nevertheless, while the knight was being so very protective of all the young ladies, but especially of his own image of perfection, he neglected his wife and son. One day, when he finally realized he needed to take off his armor and start caring for his own family, the armor had rusted from head to foot and he couldn't get it off.

He traveled to many places, searching for someone who could help him. Several blacksmiths tried their best, but even their expertise could not remove the rusty armor. He searched in vain for over a year. Finally, he found a wizard who lived in a faraway forest, surrounded by all kinds of animals. The wizard promised to help him find a solution to his problem.

Being a sophisticated gentleman, the knight found the wizard´s behavior quite ridiculous. How could such a learned man stoop to mingle with the insignificant animals in the forest? Nevertheless he befriended a little squirrel, and this humble little animal taught the important knight how to appreciate and even enjoy many of the simple things in life: the beauty of the forest, the sound of water in the brook, the perfume and beauty of the flowers, the song of a bird, the peacefulness of a sunset, and many more of God's wonders.

At the squirrel's suggestion, the knight wrote a loving letter to his son and sent it by way of Mr. Pigeon. Sad to say, the pigeon returned with a blank note from the boy and told him, "Your son told me he never had a father. He doesn't even remember what you look like. He has nothing to say".

The knight was deeply hurt and cried so much that the rust on his helmet cracked. Only then, was he able to take it off. Accompanied by his new, little friends, the knight suffered many hardships and learned to be modest, humble and conscious that he wasn't perfect after all. His sorrow and repentance were sincere and his tears cracked another section of the armor. Very slowly, piece by piece, the knight was able to free his whole body from the rusty armor.

Reading this simple fairytale, a perfect theme for a Walt Disney movie, made me reflect on my own life. After all, there was much time to meditate during those cold and endless nights of solitude. Had I really been as good a person as I believed? According to the story, everyone has some "rusty armor" in their life, and I decided it was time to get rid of mine. In my case, I didn't think my rusty armor had to do with neglecting my children. No, it wasn't that part of my life I should reflect on but I didn't have peace about my relationship with 'Mutti'. She was eighty seven when she fell and needed hip surgery. My brother 'Martin' and I decided she should live with me, so we brought her permanent maid along and hired a nurse to take care of her during the first months after her operation. This arrangement was satisfactory for 'Martin' and me, but did 'Mutti' have the privacy and quietness she needed? Reading about the Knight made me wonder how she felt about it. I loved to have my little granddaughters with me and sometimes 'Mutti' complained that they got most of my attention. I was very tolerant of the children, who were a bundle of fun, but I must admit that I had little patience for Mutti's complaints. Now

I regretted not having been more understanding. If I returned home, I would certainly try to make it up to her. I only hoped it wasn't too late.

Another issue that came to mind was the way my second marriage ended. My husband, whom I loved and admired, became a serious alcoholic about three years into our marriage. He was only a social drinker at first, but as time went by, he remained drunk most of the time. He refused help from AA or anyone else. After the last six years of his erratic behavior I couldn't take it anymore and requested a divorce.

Going back over my life, I had questions about how I handled this problem. Should I have divorced earlier, or were those last 6 years not enough? Should I have been more sensitive to his feelings, or had more respect for myself? These were my inquiries about getting rid of my own rusty armor.

Chapter 39

RADIO MESSAGES

MANUEL HAD BEEN captive for eighteen months, much longer than anyone else in our group. He knew many 'guerrilleros' from other camps where he had stayed before. One of his 'friends' brought him an old, useless radio. We were overjoyed when Franco, our handyman, managed to fix it. After making all the necessary connections and attaching two big batteries with a piece of wire, he fabricated an antenna from a wire mesh. Franco's knowledge and this old, dilapidated piece of radio put us in contact with the outside world.

Listening to the news proved that nothing had changed in Colombia. Everything was about guerrilla and paramilitary invasions, killings, kidnappings, corruption, massacres, bankruptcies, and other terrible happenings. We searched the radio stations for some encouragement and found a program called "Voces del Secuestro" (Voices to the Kidnapped) broadcasted by the government every Wednesday evening. The program was geared to the families of kidnapped people who could send their loved ones a message of hope and moral support. The response was overwhelming, and they soon extended the program to Monday and Friday evenings.

The program was encouraging because we could hear how much love these people felt for their abducted family members. But it was also discouraging to hear how many cases were still unresolved.

I wrote a note to my sons about the program and kept it in my boot, waiting for a chance to send it when the next hostage was released. It would be so encouraging to hear their loving voices of reassurance telling me they were doing everything in their power to attain my freedom.

Manuel was the first one in our group to hear a message from his wife. The second was Federico. From then on, every week someone else in our group began to receive a message from his family. We all wept when we heard Augusto's ten-year old daughter say, "Daddy, I love you so much. Every day I pray that you will come back soon. Michín (the cat) also sends you many kisses." When her little brother spoke, he couldn't stop crying and was cut off.

We often heard messages for 'Marcelo' and 'Estela'. Their sisters and cousins frequently comforted them with good news about their children. Several weeks went by without a message for me. I was very sad. I knew that my sons didn't live in Bogotá, and couldn't possibly know about the program, but down deep, it hurt to hear the loving messages for other people. 'Federico' was suddenly sent home and I had the opportunity to send my note.

I had been captive three and a half months when two days after Federico delivered my note, I heard my first radio messages from David, Alejandro and Ricardo. Later, when I was free, David told me the Chairman of the Comité, Captain Perez, had advised them to keep my profile low by never mentioning my foreign name.

But by the time they received my note, the negotiation was already quite advanced and they knew how much it would encourage me to hear their voices coming from that little radio.

"Mamita," said David, "things are looking up! Don't worry; we will have you back home very soon." Those were the most wonderful words I ever heard! Then Alejandro sent a recorded message that Ricardo brought to the station on that same Wednesday evening. Both of them sent words of encouragement and it was wonderful to hear their loving voices! I felt God's blessings and cried for joy.

Mutti's message was, "Myriam, we are praying to get you back very soon. Don't worry about me—I'm waiting for you". My companions couldn't believe that she was ninety-two years old and was still so bright and sensible, with her slight German accent.

Augusto, Victor and Manuel listened to a similar radio program on Saturdays that lasted from midnight until four a.m. These messages were targeting five hundred soldiers and policemen held as 'prisoners of war' by the FARC for over ten years in a huge barbed wire cage, somewhere in the jungle. I knew none of these messages would be for me, so I stayed in my tent and tried to get some sleep.

Meanwhile, in Bogotá:

Charlie didn't call David during the next three weeks. His silence caused tension in my family and the Comité. David called him several times but he was impossible to reach.

Captain Perez contacted a woman by the name of Eugenia who lived in a town not very far from the 'Zona de Distensión'. Several years before, her father was killed during a FARC attempt to kidnap him. From then on, Eugenia helped whenever she could and knew somebody at the 'Zona de Distensión' who might pass on some information. Since she was traveling there in an attempt to help liberate a hostage, he asked Eugenia to speak to FARC Comandante Buendía on my behalf. She promised to do so.

Chapter 40

KIDNAPPED CHILDREN

We were listening to the news one morning when we heard one of the FARC's 'most important commanders', 'Mono Jojoy', in an interview during the Peace Negotiation. He impudently lied when he said the FARC were not kidnapping children. He also denied that they were using the Demilitarized Zone to hide some of their 'economic hostages'.

Most of us had read a report by 'País Libre', the government anti-kidnapping program, telling of 176 children that were kidnapped in Colombia the past year, and some were still in the hands of the FARC. Babies were ripped from their strollers and others snatched from their mother's arms. Some were forced out of their school buses in the presence of their schoolmates.

A few children were murdered because their distraught parents were unable to pay the outrageous ransom. It was heartbreaking to hear young mothers being interviewed on a radio program, pleading for a lower ransom. A grief-stricken young mother begged for permission to send her four-year old daughter, her Teddy Bear.

We heard the poignant story of a ten-year-old boy, who was the leader in his class. This brave little boy wrote a letter to Tirofijo, asking him to "PLEASE

LEAVE THE CHILDREN OUT OF YOUR FIGHT". The FARC located the boy, dragged him out of his school bus, and held him captive for over a year. The family left the country to live in Canada as soon as he was free.

One day two 'guerrilleros' were taking a small kidnapped boy from one camp to another. They stopped to eat at ours on their way. When I asked the little boy his name and how old he was, he answered, "Alexander", and held up three little fingers, the way very young children do. He was shivering and eating his dry pasta with appetite. Alexander reminded me of my little grandson, Billy. Last time I had seen Billy, he was four years old. When I took him and his sister Marcela to the zoo and we were watching the caged monkeys, Billy told me, "Omi, why are these poor monkeys locked up?" I was amazed that such a young child could understand the monkey's need for freedom. Sandra brought me back to reality and shooed me away from the little boy. I went to my tent and cried.

The next day we heard on the radio that a small boy was kidnapped in Victor's hometown. When Victor heard the father's name, he told us he was one of his best childhood friends. Victor became even more depressed, knowing there was nothing he could do to help this adorable child get back to his parents.

Chapter 41

CHILD GUERRILLEROS

EVERY DAY, ONE or two different groups of bandits stopped by our camp on their journey to another camp. They were usually running errands, bringing food from the 'Compañía' to the small camps, accompanying new kidnapped people, or delivering messages to the commanders. Sometimes a couple of subversives would pick up one or two hostages and take them to the mountain peak, 'Telecom', to communicate by radio-phone with their families, for proof of life.

A young 'guerrillero' caught my attention—there was something refined about this boy. He looked more like a city teenager. He hardly spoke to anybody and it was easy to sense that he didn't fit in with the others. Once, I tried to strike up a conversation with him, but refrained when I realized that he felt uncomfortable. He was obviously there against his will. Most likely, he ran away from home, enlisted in the FARC, and was now aware of his mistake. I'll never forget the melancholy look in this boy's green eyes. It was sad that I had no way to help him, but any friendly gesture between the boy and a hostage would be noticed. His parents must have been devastated.

Perhaps the most shocking aspect of the guerrilla movement was the number of children fighting in their ranks. Some joined the FARC because they were attracted by the glamour of carrying a gun, receiving a salary, or earning a position of what they thought would be 'respect'. Others were enlisted by force under the threat that their parents would be killed if they didn't. Some joined out of hunger, to have clothes to wear, or simply for the excitement of belonging to a group.

Many children who run away from home become easy prey for the subversives, who are always eager to enlist them. Two weeks after they enter the ranks, they are given an opportunity to change their minds and leave—much too soon to know how brutal their lives will turn out to be. If they miss this opportunity, never again will they be able to return to their families and a normal civilian life.

Children from poor villages are impressionable and easy to recruit. They are instructed in the ways of terrorism and become efficient and remorseless killers. Often they are forced to commit atrocities they don't fully understand, in the name of 'the cause'. They are sent as cannon fodder to fight on the front lines, leading the militia´s advances ahead of the older troops. Those who don't have a fierce character and might have guilty feelings about their crimes are fed small amounts of gunpowder in their food, which turns them into ruthless mercenaries. This is how peasants enhance the viciousness of their watchdogs. Some peasant families with more education often have relatives living in the cities. In order to save their children from this tragic destiny, they will send them off to live for years with these relatives. Nevertheless, when they reach the cities, they are exposed to many dangers. Opportunities to study are limited and many fall into drugs or prostitution.

When the Army wins a confrontation, the youngest guerrillas end up wounded on the field. They are taken to "Bienestar Familiar," the Family

Welfare Services, and given a chance to be guided towards a new life. Much effort is being made to rehabilitate these damaged youngsters. The process is slow, and the need is great. It takes time, psychological attention, and much care to recuperate them from such a wicked childhood.

These youngsters are thrust into a morally deprived environment at a very susceptible age. Feelings of real love among the subversives are cautiously dealt with by their superiors. When a young couple falls in love they are separated because females are considered 'property' of the FARC, mainly for the pleasure of their leaders.

Long ago, in a conversation I had with the mother of a large peasant family, she vaguely spoke of her son who was in the Colombian Army. However, she seemed particularly proud of another son who had joined the guerrilla. Even though she had lost him to the FARC, she had a glorified idea that he was now important. She spoke proudly, similar to a parent whose son was recently accepted to West Point.

*   *   *   *   *   *

Sandra told me a sad story about a thirteen year old guerrilla girl who became pregnant when she was 'serving' the old guys at the 'Compañía'. She shot herself, but she didn't die then. They didn't take her to a hospital—they let her suffer a slow and painful agony till she died.

One day I asked William, "Do you want your children to follow in your footsteps and someday join the guerrilla forces?" He didn't answer with words, but his eyes clouded over and I could sense his sadness.

The respect and admiration some peasants used to have for the FARC and the Paramilitaries had been transformed into terror when they realized that not only the wealthy, upper, and middle class, but also the poor, are being attacked by the bandits.

Chapter 42

VICTOR

VERY EARLY ONE morning, Victor was escorted to the top of 'Telecom' mountain to talk to Liliana, his wife, on the radio-phone. When he returned to the camp that evening, he was overjoyed by the excellent news. She had reached an agreement on the amount for the ransom and had found a buyer for their home and their car. She needed to hear Victor's voice as proof of life, to sell the house and pay the ransom to the FARC. In only one week, Victor would be released and sent back to his family! He promised to contact our families immediately. He was the Director of the hospital in his city, and promised to send an ambulance to pick each of us up when he was informed that we were to go free.

What happened next was devastating! The FARC kept silent for two months. The rumour was that the 'chulos' (Army vultures) were surrounding us. Victor knew the FARC tactics, that this was only an excuse to stall the closure of the negotiation. He fell into a deep depression. He was sure 'Liliana' had sold everything they owned to make this payment; there was nothing left to sell. But all the signs indicated that the FARC were going to make a second demand.

Victor had been an excellent companion and was well liked by everyone. It was very sad to see him fall apart like that. He never played cards with us again, and we couldn't get him to speak or eat. Whenever I brought him some rice and lentils, he would say something like, "I'm fasting today, but I'll eat tomorrow." He lost much weight—you could hardly see his face under his bushy, black, curly hair and beard. He had been the kindest and strongest person in our group, and it was painful to see him now. He had gone out of his way to treat the 'guerrilleros' when they were sick, and yet he received no preferential treatment.

Chapter 43

CAPTIVES' STATUS

THE 'COMPAÑÍA' WAS a big camp of approximately eighty tents that housed about two hundred 'guerrilleros'. Three or four commanders lived there with a doctor and a dentist to attend FARC members. Most of their main activities took place there, including terrorist training and negotiators dealing with the families of the 'economic hostages'. We were not allowed to go to there and whenever one of us asked to speak to a higher 'comandante', the answer was always, "Mañana". We never had the 'honor' of meeting the top brass.

There were a few minor differences regarding the living conditions in the nine camps in our area. The variations depended on how much money the victims were worth to the bandits. The important ones, who were considered 'political trophies', got slightly better food and lodging than the unimportant groups such as ours—nevertheless, they were held for many years as leverage for future negotiations.

Often, they are cruelly chained to a tree or to another kidnapped person, or even worse, completely isolated from contact with other hostages. They are sometimes tortured to extract information about their properties, or the properties of others, who will be the FARC's next target. This caliber of hostage is held in captivity for a much longer period of time. Three American men were there for six years.

A hostage who was chained to a pole and left alone the entire nine months of his captivity, lost his mind and died shortly after he was set free.

Judging by the food we were 'served', we figured we only qualified as one of the many groups of less importance. We were never blessed with a fruit, a vegetable, an egg, or even a slice of bread—much less a piece of cake or a piece of chicken. I heard Faber say. "Those #$%@&*'cuchos' are so broke, they don't even deserve the slush they gobble up."

By doing simple math, we figured the FARC were spending one thousand five hundred pesos daily to feed us three meals of rice and lentils, and two snacks of 'aguapanela' with crushed saltines. This was the equivalent of fifty U.S. cents (0.50) per day, per person. Every 'guest' was expected to return his uniform, boots and blanket when he was released, to be passed on and 'enjoyed' by the next 'guest'. The FARC was certainly not investing much on our behalf.

Augusto, Victor and I were sitting on the straw in my tent one morning when William brought a cabbage to the camp. This was the only vegetable we had laid eyes on in months. "We're getting coleslaw tonight! Hopefully, Sandra will throw in a few pieces of pineapple!" someone said. This was, of course, only wishful thinking. To our dismay, our captors used the cabbage to play soccer in the mud!

One day I shared my thoughts on the 'camp cuisine' with Claudio, "For a tastier and well balanced diet, why not feed us dog chow? It would be easier, more appealing, and more hygienic to serve."

I could tell from the expression on his face that my comment didn't go over too well. Nevertheless, upsetting him was one of the very few pleasures available to me. *"Careful Myriam, better watch your tongue",* I reminded myself.

*   *   *   *   *   *

About nine more weeks went by and nobody else was liberated. We were all getting anxious. Alone, on those sleepless, icy and damp nights, I couldn't help worrying about my future.

I prayed, "Dear God, please don't forget us. By the time we get out of here, we'll probably be sick and looking and feeling about a hundred years old. Not only that, but if our loved ones are finally able to pay the ransom, everyone will be broke."

After working so hard for twenty-six years at 'Buganviles' and decorating dozens of gardens, my hope was to have a comfortable, old age without being a burden to my hard-working sons. However, things looked quite miserable for me now. I hoped that our two properties in Bogotá were rented.

*   *   *   *   *   *

On his journey to the 'campamento', Franco noticed a plant called 'vira-vira', growing on the next mountain. He was allowed to pick these leaves once a week to make a beverage that was supposed to cure urinary problems. Most of us drank it in the mornings and evenings but I soon realized that it made me get up too many times at night and I stopped taking it in the evenings. Rafael said, "I don't need 'vira-vira' or anything else. The doctor says I am so virile I can exhaust twenty women every day!" Our super-macho idiot received a standing applause.

*   *   *   *   *   *

'Marcelo' and 'Estela' sadly told us their tenth wedding anniversary was the next day. They had already invited all their friends and relatives to a party.

In the afternoon, on Franco's search for 'vira-vira' leaves, he came across an area covered with beautiful mountain flowers. From his description, it was similar to the rain forest I passed on my way to the first camp. Franco picked an arm-full of wild flowers and leaves, brought them to the camp, and we all participated in making a flower arrangement for Estela and Marcelo. We used a piece of wire to attach 'frailejón' leaves to a moss-covered branch and added on the mountain flowers. Under the circumstances, our homemade flower arrangement meant more than the most expensive gift, even though the day was grey and rainy and the food was as lousy as always.

*   *   *   *   *   *

Meanwhile in Bogotá:

After a long wait, a FARC bandit, who identified himself as 'Boa', called David. He announced that Charlie was dead and he was taking on the negotiation. The 'Comité' was relieved to reassume contact with the FARC.

When they were getting along reasonably well, David and 'Boa' referred to each other as 'bro'. But when Boa was mean, David used the same offensive language as his opponent just as he had done with 'Charlie'. Once, David even yelled, "Forget it, you son of a bitch!" and hung up on him.

A few days later, when Boa called again, David told him, "Hey bro, the guys already sold the car and also wanna sign over the farm to the FARC as part of the ransom."

"Ya better move fast or ya'll get the 'cucha' back in a black plastic bag. And ya don't want ta know what they'll do to her before they stick her in there . . . I'll ask the boss if they wanna accept the farm as part of the dough," he answered.

A few days later Boa called back and told David the answer was NO. The farm had to be sold to someone else. "The FARC already own enough land, and they want CASH!" He added, "Besides, that whole area is 'salted' (cursed) anyway".

David said, "Come on man, do you think anybody will buy a farm where someone was kidnapped?" Boa replied coldly, "Too bad, man, that's yar problem."

Boa was definitely tougher than Charlie and he tried David's patience to the limit. After battling with this evil, hostile specimen over the phone one day, his steel nerves were shot. When David ended a discussion with 'Boa' he hung up and couldn't help but burst out crying. The 'Comité' was very supportive of him. They knew how difficult it was for David to be negotiating my life for money.

Chapter 44

FOREIGNERS

ONE EVENING TWO 'guerrilleros' from another camp dropped off an elderly gentleman who spoke Spanish with a strong German accent. Gunther was deeply affected by the fact that his friend, who was captured with him, had been shot before his eyes by some maniac whose only explanation was, "I didn't like him."

During his first week at the camp it was difficult to get Gunther to speak to anyone. Being in the hands of those savages was too much for him. All he wanted was to die quickly, knowing he would never return to his family alive. We all tried to encourage him not to give up, but he was deeply depressed and nothing we said seemed to help.

We heard on the radio that, among the three-and-a-half thousand people kidnapped in Colombia each year, approximately ten percent were foreigners. Their Ambassadors try to help through 'diplomatic channels'. Needless to say, an Ambassador will never consider negotiating a ransom with terrorists, while a parent or a son will do anything, even pay an extortion, to save their loved one's life.

It is a known fact that the FARC bandits had orders to shoot their kidnapped victims whenever the Army attempted a rescue mission. If the victims were kept within the 'demilitarized zone' such an attempt was out of question.

Our captors spoke of a Japanese gentleman who was being held in another camp. His company had kidnapping insurance coverage for their employees. Being insured is a drawback for the victim because, when the bandits know that a person is covered by insurance, they insist on their initial demand and refuse to budge. This increases the time of agony and makes the negotiation process even more frustrating.

After eighteen months of captivity, the Japanese gentleman was liberated when his company paid an enormous sum. But the worst was yet to come. He traveled to live in Japan, and returned to Colombia two years later to sell some properties he still owned in Bogotá. A few days after his arrival he was kidnapped a second time, and if he is alive, he is probably still in the hands of the terrorists.

It took Gunther a week to even venture out of his tent. Very slowly, Augusto managed to persuade him to interact with us. At around that time, Manuel, who had been there longer than anyone else in our group, was sent to freedom. It was encouraging to all of us, especially to Gunther, who hadn't witnessed anyone's departure so far.

Manuel's farewell was very emotional. He had been a bridge of understanding between the bandits and us. There was tension in the air because we didn't know if he was really being sent home or not. Even Faber, Alacrán's apprentice, cried.

Chapter 45

ARMANDO AND ESPERANZA

PANCHITA AND I were washing our clothes at Methuselah's pond when we were approached by a man we hadn't seen before. He was crying. He was a tall man in his late forties and his appearance disclosed his hellish experience, just like everyone else who recently arrived. He introduced himself as 'Armando'. He and his wife had just arrived at the camp after a four-day journey from Ibagué, their home town. Luckily their children, who were ten and twelve, had stayed home with their grandparents that day.

Armando said, "I can't understand why they kidnapped us. Even though we don't agree with the FARC, for security reasons, we have been paying them a monthly extortion fee over the past four years." He showed us a laminated card that proved he was a FARC 'contributor'. When the captors saw his 'carnet', they told him they were only following orders. "The patron might send ya back when he sees yar card".

When we returned to the tents, Armando introduced us to his wife, 'Esperanza'. She had fallen off the horse on the fourth day of their journey and was in great pain. She was a heavy-set woman and except for a few wool socks and a T-shirt, there was nothing available in the camp that fit her. The camouflaged uniforms were about four sizes too small and this made her feel even worse.

I visited Esperanza every day and we talked for hours. She came from a very rich family on the northern coast of Colombia. She told me that despite the high extortion fee her father had paid, he was kidnapped six years earlier and his body was sent home in a black, plastic bag. When two of her brothers were threatened, they left their businesses and other properties and migrated to Ecuador with their families. Her story increased my anxiety. While crossing the mountains to get here, they slept at a FARC encampment where they saw a fellow who used to work at her family's hardware store, and was fired because he broke into the cash register. He must have been the one to tell the FARC where to find Armando and Esperanza.

This made me wonder how my kidnappers learned that I was at Buganviles early that fatal Tuesday morning, when I had been absent for several weeks. Who could have told them? No, Jaider and Gladys would never do this to me. After eighteen years of a good and easy life at our farm, they would never betray me. They were envied by others in the neighborhood because of their lucky situation. But then, could they have been tempted by a good amount of money and a promise they would be owners of the farm? Could these thoughts have gone through their heads? They would have known that even if I returned to freedom, I would never set foot on Buganviles again, and since it was impossible to sell any farm at that time, it would have to be practically given away.

I remembered my twenty-six years of hard work at 'Buganviles' and the joy it brought me. It was painful to suspect people who were so dear to me. But on the other hand, I would never go back there and holding on to the past wouldn´t let me look ahead. Would I ever find out the truth? Anyone in the neighboring town could have been the guilty party.

*   *   *   *   *   *

FARC DECREE 002

The FARC became shamelessly bold, and claimed the right to demand 'taxes' from most Colombian and foreign companies operating in the country.

Their decree states:

"Every commercial business in Colombia with assets adding up to one million dollars or more must pay taxes to the Colombian Revolutionary Armed Forces, FARC. Any President of a company or important official who doesn't comply with this law is at risk of being captured."

According to El Tiempo, dated April 25, 2003, the rate of kidnappings during the first months of the year decreased somewhat. Nevertheless, this good news camouflaged a macabre increase in the number of extortions targeting Colombian and foreign businessmen.

The lack of security reigning in the country at this time forced the frightened population to give in to the FARC's threats.

The following is a translation of one of the extortion letters that many small business owners received:

53rd Unit of the Revolutionary Armed Forces of Colombia—Pursuing our Cause for a Free Nation

Subject: Taxes
From: The Supreme FARC Authorities

Greetings. This is to inform you that Decree 002 has come into effect and you are expected to comply.

You will soon receive instructions regarding the specific location where, and the date when you are expected to appear. To avoid being cheated by people who are not members of our Organization, it is of utmost importance that you follow through with these instructions to the detail. All of our negotiations take place at our camps, located in rural areas.

IF YOU DO NOT COMPLY, CONSIDER YOURSELF ONE OF THE FARC'S MILITARY TARGETS.

Of course, these letters always caused panic and things became more complicated when the Government sent Police to guard the roadways leading to the guerrilla camps, preventing the delegates of these companies from reaching the meeting places. When they couldn't submit their 'taxes', they returned to the city with the bitter feeling that the FARC would keep them listed as targets for future kidnappings.

Regrettably, these methods of extortion turned into a lucrative, criminal industry. Some guerrilla camps became busy 'cashier booths' where enormous sums were collected from the terrified 'contributors' who followed through with the payoff, hoping to be spared. However, even after they paid up, they knew this was probably only the first time around, and they were destined to live with on-going fear.

A Spanish family who had worked very hard during five decades in Colombia and owned a restaurant in an elegant neighbourhood in Bogota received one of these extortion letters. Out of principle, they decided to ignore the threat. A few days later, the whole area was rocked by a deafening explosion. The terrorists placed a bomb inside the restaurant, killing nine people, wounding others, and leaving the building in shambles. The ruins of the restaurant stood as a declaration of war to all those who refuse to pay extortions. The family lost everything they had worked for and returned to Spain.

Chapter 46

URINE THERAPY

ONE RAINY MORNING, 'Federico' asked 'Alacrán' to lend us his playing cards. We played a game called 'Fooling your Neighbor.' The way to win was to get rid of all your cards. The person left with the most cards in his hand loses the game.

It must have been the stress that provoked some players to be aggressive and childish, making fun of the loser. To make matters worse, the 'guerrilleros' wanted to know exactly who lost every game and in their primitive and rude manner, they joined in to taunt that person. I lost twice. My fragile state of mind prevented me from being a good sport. I decided not to lose again. Before I knew it, I found myself cheating. I didn't want to be 'the pig' for a third time in a row, so I slipped two cards into my pocket.

As fate would have it, when Federico returned the deck of cards, Alacrán counted them and noticed that two were missing.

"How'bout that! Someone here isn't an honest person! Dont'cha think ya're gonna git'way with it! We're gonna search ta find out!!" he announced.

I was petrified! I remembered an incident at the first camp when two tuna fish cans were missing. They searched in our tents and found the two cans among Pedro's things. They chained him to a pole for two weeks.

Fortunately, Federico knew I had the two cards in my pocket. He talked Alacrán into letting us play again that afternoon, giving me a chance to return them without being noticed. I was so relieved.

*　　*　　*　　*　　*　　*

Franco, our handy-man, who knew about alternative medicine, came up with a theory unknown to most of us.

"I know this doesn't sound appealing—but, since we're not getting our daily medicine, it might be advisable for some of us to try an oriental practice called 'Urine Therapy'. Drinking an ounce of one's own first urine every morning supposedly strengthens the immune system and keeps one healthy under adverse conditions. I'm willing to try it," he said.

I asked Victor for his professional opinion on the matter.

He told me, "Well, under normal circumstances I wouldn't prescribe it to my patients—but I've read that some oriental cultures practice Urine Therapy to prevent arthritis and other illnesses when there is no traditional medication available."

The Osteoarthritis in my hands was increasing but I couldn't decide which was worse; the pain or drinking urine. It was repulsive to me! Most of us refused to consider it an option but as time passed not only Franco, but also Mauricio and Teresa admitted they were getting satisfactory results. I slowly allowed Franco's suggestion to creep into my mind.

How low could one get? I remembered my recent appearance in the mirror, which was humiliating enough. Being held prisoner by these ruffians and living according to their rules like an animal was lower than one could imagine. Now, on top of it all, the thought of starting off the day drinking urine added more anguish to my pathetic situation! I waited about a week, gave it a thought every day, and always decided against it. Nevertheless, since the joints in my fingers were swelling and aching more and more, I let the repulsive thought linger in my mind. Soon, I found myself searching in the mud for that important, and evasive plastic bottle I had my eye on, but had tried to ignore. When I found the bottle, I washed it and asked Franco to cut it in half. Then I left it in my bag of treasures. Maybe one morning I would have the nerve to go ahead with the project.

I had been captive for over four months now and, even though I was certain that my sons were doing their best, I had no idea how things were going. The days dragged by endlessly and anxiety was killing me, little by little.

There were times when I was sure I would survive and be sent back to freedom, someday. But other times my faith wavered, and I had the feeling everything was static and I was doomed to remain there forever. I wanted my friends to know me as a courageous and positive person, but the truth was I was very weak and at times, discouraged. What an effort it was to get up every day and go through the motions! I remembered Federico's words of reassurance that he repeated once in a while to each of us.

"Myriam, remember that we are in a zero-star hotel and if we stay long enough, the bill will slowly go down to a sum our family can afford. If they pay the ransom too quickly, the FARC will assume their demand was too low. They hold on to the hostage and stay silent for several months. Then, when they have stretched the family's nerves to the limit, they make another demand and the struggle to get the money for the second ransom begins." This was Victor's situation. It is estimated that twenty percent of the families have to pay a second ransom—and some even three times before they get their loved one back. Others, not even then . . .

Over four months had passed when two bandits from the main camp came to talk to me. They brought a notebook and asked the same questions about my finances I had answered on my third day at the first camp.

When I told them I had answered these questions to Simón at the first camp, one of them said, "The patrón said ta git that shit again 'cause the ol'ones faded in't mud." Whether the notebook had faded into the mud or not was irrelevant. The worst part was the frustration of knowing they had lost so much time and were just now taking on my case. All my answers were the same as before.

Chapter 47

PROOF OF LIFE

EARLY ONE MORNING, two 'guerrilleros' from another camp came to guide Augusto and me to the highest peak in the area they called 'Telecom'. The negotiation could only go forward if someone from our families heard our voices for 'proof of life'.

Before I left, Federico gave me a small, plastic bottle to fill up in the streams along the way to stay hydrated. We started our long journey after breakfast and walked endlessly, circling upwards around the mountain. We jumped from one rock to another while crossing several brooks and waded into two large rivers with strong currents. We ended up swimming to get to the other side.

Augusto was my guardian angel. He convinced Milton and Pepe, the 'guerrilleros' leading us, to stop for a few minutes when I was tired, and gave me his hand to help me over many obstacles on the way.

We passed by the Compañía and briefly saw the 'guerrilleros' in their daily activities. Some were cleaning their guns, others were washing clothes—but most of them were just standing around, doing nothing.

Milton proudly stated, "Last night we had a big party at the Compañia—everybody got drunk." When we got back to the camp we heard on the radio that the FARC had attacked a small town and killed forty-two people.

After six hours of strenuous walking I could hardly continue. I heard the younger guerrillero say, "That $%#@&* cucha ain´t gonna make it!"

This made Augusto and I even more determined to continue. We knew that our freedom depended on this call, so with his help and encouragement, I mustered up every bit of strength and plodded on.

An hour later Milton pointed to the peak of the next mountain; this was 'Telecom'. When I looked up, my heart almost stopped. There, squarely in front of us, stood a gigantic cliff of flat, vertical rocks, rising into the sky like the facade of a twelve story building.

How was I ever going to make it to the top? There were hardly any branches to hold on to, and only a few sparse ledges to rest a foot. It seemed impossible; however, we needed to try, and begged God for His help.

Augusto climbed ahead of me and then turned to grab my hand, pulling me up and across each enormous slate of rock. I was optimistic and climbed for several hours with his help. My heart was beating frantically and as we were getting closer to the top, breathing became more difficult. My strength was failing and I feared I would slide back down into nothingness. Somehow, after that endless struggle we reached the peak! My head was spinning and I collapsed. Certainly, I could never have accomplished such a 'tour de force' without Augusto's indispensable support.

Five FARC bandits, armed with grenade-launchers, were sitting in a fox hole waiting for airplanes to fly over the area to shoot them down. It was a desolate, barren place, with no protection from the wind. Only the guerilleros and the ever present hawks could survive there.

Augusto called out, "Myriam, come and take a look at this spectacular view."

I was too exhausted and breathless to care about the view. Milton dialled a number and pushed the phone into my hand.

At the sound of David's voice my heart began pounding even harder. I was crying when David calmly told me, "Mrs. Myriam, we've never met—I'm a friend of your son David. My name is Gustavo Alvarez, and I'm in charge of the negotiation for your release. I need to confirm the names of your aunt and uncle to make sure I´m negotiating for the right person."

"Fritz and Wally," I said, my voice trembling.

I had to control my emotions. I asked how my family was and sent them my love. He replied, "They are in good health and they love you very much. We are negotiating, and hopefully you'll be getting home soon. Please be patient, Mrs. Myriam, it won't take too much longer."

Milton pulled the phone from my hand and yelled, "Ya better git that money fast! This @#$%^& old hag's very sick, and if we don't git that dough soon, she'll have ta die!"

Then Milton called Augusto's wife and let him talk to her for a few seconds. He pulled the phone from Augusto's hand and yelled, "That Son of a bitch's got two brok'n ribs. If ya don't want'im back in a black bag, ya b'tter send that do'gh fast!"

Climbing down the stone-mountain was even more distressful. I perched on every narrow, little ledge along the face of the cliff, sliding carefully from one to the next, gripping on to Augusto's hand. We determined not to look down from the precipice. A slight mistake or slip of the foot could have meant certain death for both of us. My nerves were in pieces by the time I reached solid ground.

After we had conquered that most dangerous leg of the journey, the rest seemed easy. Four additional hours of fast walking awaited us before we arrived at camp. We had overcome another hair-raising episode and although we were exhausted, we thanked God for the miracle of bringing us back alive.

Claudio asked me, "What did yar son say?"

"I spoke with a negotiator—not my son."

"FARC's big bosses don't like ta deal with negotat'rs. It's better if yar fam'ly talks." I thought to myself, "Sure, you creep! You won't be able to manipulate us much longer!"

I fell on my back on the hay in my tent and didn't even look for the hairy, black worms. The sound of David´s voice made the longing to be with my loved ones even more acute and the tension and danger of that day robbed me of any strength I had left.

Chapter 48

FINALLY!!!

BACK IN BOGOTÁ:

No progress was being made so David told 'Boa', "Hey man, since we're not getting anywhere, and I'm just wasting my time, I'm gonna quit. I mean, I don't even know the woman. So, do what ya want, bro—I'm quittin!"

As hard as it was for David to say this, it helped to untangle the negotiation. 'Boa' started to call him every other day. Gradually, David began to raise the offer, but 'Boa' still refused to budge. After five months, 'Boa' seemed to soften up and slowly began to lower the ransom.

When the two negotiators seemed to get along rather well and some progress was achieved, they ended their conversation in the classiest FARC manner: "Palabra de gallero!" Meaning, A 'cock-fighter's word of honor' or a 'gentleman's agreement' which of course, in FARC ethical context doesn't mean a thing. Anyway, David considered it a step forward.

After many stressful calls involving endless haggling, David and 'Boa' came to an agreement. 'Boa' called a few days later and told David the date, time and place of the 'transaction'. Someone representing the family was to deliver the ransom to this place and after counting the money, the FARC would set me free.

When he was informed of my kidnapping at the start, Jaime, my favourite nephew on Hernando's side, offered to cooperate with David in every possible way. He knew that direct relatives are not supposed to pick up their loved ones in captivity, so he told David to call him when it was time. He and his friend, 'Julio', were willing to take the risk.

'Boa' called David once again and demanded a list of items; mainly radio phones, power saws and boots, which could be included as part of the payment. From past experience, Captain Perez knew that sending these items could delay the 'transaction'. Our captors, looking for ways to stall, would complain that the radios were not working, or they weren't the kind they wanted, or the boots were not the right sizes, etc. The 'Comité' agreed that it was safer to stick to cash and keep things as fast and simple as possible.

Captain Perez advised my sons not to enter the FARC region. The members of the 'Comité' had a strict policy to meet whoever was going to do the pickup. After they interviewed Jaime and Julio, they agreed that these two young men met all the requirements. They were brave, reliable, and not directly related to me. Despite the danger, Jaime and Julio were courageous enough to enter FARC territory carrying a large amount of cash. If everything worked out as planned, they would bring me home.

Chapter 49

AM I DREAMING?

Saturday morning, at the camp:

As the saying goes, "The darkest hour comes before dawn." I never had a chance to find out if the 'urine therapy' works or not. I was unprepared when what I had wished for the most, finally came to pass. One morning at five, Claudio approached my tent and woke me up to the following words, "Git ready, ya're leavin!" I couldn't believe my ears. "Can you please repeat that?" I asked.

"Ya're leavin!" he yelled.

First I thought it must be a mistake. Victor had been there so much longer than I, and yet there was no sign of his release. Could it be true? The wonderful news sank in. "Thank You, thank You, thank You so much, my Dear God!"

All I had to do was put on my boots and I was ready in an instant. I felt their sincerity as my friends gathered outside my tent to wish me luck. It was always such a joy when someone was sent to freedom! The only thing that clouded my happiness at this glorious moment was to know they were staying behind. Each one gave me a note for his family which I hid in my socks and promised to deliver in person.

I left my 'sleeping bag', T-shirts and socks to 'Esperanza', my gloves to 'Panchita', and my solitaire to 'Augusto'. When he saw I was giving everything away, Augusto advised me to hold on to the boots because the journey ahead could be very tough. I appreciated his advice when I faced the endless kilometers of mud on the mountain. 'Augusto' made me a 'poncho' out of a piece of plastic to protect me from the rain. 'Armando' tied a plastic bag to each side of a string to hang my shoes over my neck in case I was not allowed to use the boots for the journey.

"You'll need your hands free to help you climb", he said.

I was worried about Victor's depression. He didn't come out of his tent so I went to say fare-well to him and get his note for his family.

"I didn't write a note. Please call 'Liliana' and tell her I love her and our children," he said.

As usual, we all held hands and thanked God for my release. 'Augusto' and 'Panchita' accompanied me to the 'rancha' to get some breakfast but Faber, who was on cooking duty that day, hadn't even started to build a fire. The only thing available was some 'aguapanela' left over from the day before.

"Ya won't git nothin!" he said. He was punishing me because the evening before I had refused to eat the sardines from a can they opened two days earlier.

Two 'guerrilleros' I hadn't seen before came to escort me. They told me the pickup place was at what they called 'the pink house' where someone would take me and drop me off at a bus stop for Bogotá. Our captors were having 'almojábanas' with their 'aguapanela', but such a luxury was never offered to us. The rice and lentils would be ready in an hour, and we had to leave immediately but I was so happy, nothing mattered. I said a tearful farewell to my companions and looked for 'Claudio', 'Sandra' and 'William' to say good bye. They were friendly and gave me the "see ya soon" look. God forbid! I was pleased to see that 'Alacrán' and 'Raquel' weren't around.

Now I was ready to start climbing the mountain. My escorts were 'Camilo', about fifteen, and 'Jezid', a few years older. 'Camilo' never said a word. The morning was foggy as usual, and we could only see about eight feet ahead. We started our journey through the wilderness. There were no trails to follow. We were crawling up the mountain, and I often needed to stop and catch my breath.

'Jezid' said, "Ya'll have ta walk fast 'cos we got ta git ta the pink house ba noon. A car will take ya to a town were ya can catch a bus. They'll even give ya twelve thous'nd pesos for the bus. If ya're not there by two, the driver "se delica" (will get pissed off) and will leave without ya.

We reached what seemed to be a fringe of brown mud, similar to my journey on horseback to the first camp. 'Jezid' proudly told me that the FARC was building this 'road' to connect their over 180 'retention camps', all over the country. A broken down bulldozer was the only sign something was being accomplished. It was just a long strip of deep, brown sludge. But I was so happy, everything I saw seemed beautiful.

'Jezid' was constantly communicating on the radio with someone who was always telling him to hurry up. I literally had to pull my enormous boots out of the sludge at each step. I slipped and fell several times. We had been walking for three hours and were making little progress.

When 'Jezid' told me for the tenth time to hurry up, I answered, "Believe me, I'm even more anxious than you are to reach that pink house. I beg you to call and ask if we could get a horse to speed up our journey."

The temperature must have been in the low thirties and the fog was very dense. As usual, it was raining. However, my heart was bubbling with joy!

'Jezid' called to ask for a horse. The answer was "ni pu'el putas," (!@#$%^%&* for 'no way'). I knew this was practically impossible because there wasn't a living creature within hundreds of miles. I prayed, "Dear God, I beg you to send me a horse. I will never make it without Your help!"

I had reached the limit of my strength and was digging my booted foot out of the mud when I looked up and there were two peasant men on horses, right in front of me. I hadn´t heard them approach—they appeared out of the fog like a miracle. 'Jezid' ordered the men to continue their journey on one horse. They could pick the other one up a few days later at a place they agreed on. One of the men got off his horse, mounted the other one, and they rode away. I thanked them and mounted the horse. Again, it was evident that the peasants, out of fear, are forced to obey commands from any armed FARC member.

Five months had gone by since I had seen anyone who wasn't a 'guerrillero' or a kidnapped person. Neither had I seen an animal, aside from the hawks and the little rabbit. We didn't run into any other living creature that whole day while crossing the mountain range.

Occasionally, the horse got stuck in the mud but always managed to free itself. I had been on the horse for more than five additional hours when I asked 'Jezid' if we were getting close.

"Ya need six more hours, that´s if ya move fast enough". I knew enough not to believe a word that came from a 'guerrillero'.

Just as on my first journey, I rode on mountain trails that bordered precipices, crossed streams and rivers. The rocks were slippery, and the horse and I sank into the cold water several times. But this time I was so happy, nothing bothered me. From time to time we ended up back on the muddy road project, and then returned to another slippery trail bordering another precipice.

I had been riding for many hours when unexpectedly, my horse did something strange. Slowly, it sat down, as if courteously inviting me to get off its back—which I did. Then it turned over on its back with its legs facing the sky and began to wiggle back and forth, scratching itself in the mud. It wasn't strange for a dog to do this, but never a saddled horse. My captors laughed. Eventually, the horse got back on its feet and we continued our journey. The horse, the saddle and I were a mess, but if the horse was comfortable, I was happy.

We finally reached the other side of the mountain. The fog lifted, and below me was a beautiful valley seated peacefully between two mountain-ranges. When I saw the breath-taking view, a wonderful feeling of FREEDOM embraced me for the first time!

The scenery was absolutely magnificent. The sun was shining and the temperature was pleasant. This was my first re-encounter with the beauty of our country. It is impossible to describe my joy and excitement at the sight of those tiny houses, and patchwork squares of farmland on the distant mountains ahead. These were the first signs that we were approaching civilization.

'Jezid' called again and told me the driver was waiting for me. He could see how excited I was. When we finally reached flat terrain he told me I could ride by myself if I wanted to. I softly tapped my horse that began to gallop straight ahead. What a wonderful feeling it was to be free!!!! All my fears were gone. Thank God, I had made it!

Soon I would be hugging each member of my beloved family. I would be with my sons and daughters-in-law, my 'Mutti', and my adorable grand-children.

The next day I would see 'Martin', my sister-in-law, my niece and nephew and my friends. Yesterday I was facing the harsh fact that I would spend a desolate New Year on that dreadful mountain, and today I was FREE, AND ON MY WAY HOME!

When I stopped to rest my knees after many hours on the horse, I suddenly felt dizzy and fainted. When I came to, everything was black, I couldn't see a thing. When 'Jezid' saw my condition, I heard him call his boss, "Damn! The 'merchandise' is croakin' on us—she just went blind. What's I supposed ta do? OK, I don't have notin', but she'll git some cake". He pulled a wrapped slice of cake and a can of soda out of his pocket and gave them to me. After a little while, my eyesight was restored and I was soon back on the horse.

After what seemed like an eternity, we reached the famous pink house. It was about six thirty p.m. I looked around anxiously for the car, but it was nowhere in sight. They told me the driver had left in the morning. What was going to happen next? Did the negotiation fail? Out of nowhere, an older, sullen looking 'guerrillero' approached me, a radio phone in his hand. With an air of arrogance, he said, "I'm comandante 'Boa'. I'm the one in charge of ya."

My excitement grew when 'Boa' handed me a phone, and I heard David's voice on the other end,

"Lady, just answer my question with a YES or a NO. Are you in the same place where we talked last time?"

I answered, "NO". That was all. 'Boa' pulled the phone from my hand and walked away, talking to David. A few minutes later he came back and yelled,

"That @#$%^%$#@ family of yars sent the vultures (Army) after us. We're surrounded! I'm sendin ya back ta a camp tamorrow and ya'll stay there till ya rot!"

The horror I felt was beyond words! All my happiness dissolved in an instant. The thought of having to return to one of those ghastly camps was unbearable. I was determined not to live this nightmare all over again and decided that if I wasn't released within a month, I would find a knife or a razor blade to end my life. I regretted that in my haste I had left the broken piece of mirror behind. How easy it is to make a terrible mistake in desperate moments.

'Jezid' finally lead me to a little beer shop at the pink house where I collapsed on a wooden bench and cried. One of the men who was drinking beer, came and sat beside me, "I remember you from the day they were taking you to the 'campamento'—you stayed at our house." He looked familiar. He reminded me that his wife, 'Rosa', had given me a pair of woolen socks.

"What did they do to you?—you were a good-looking lady, and now you look like a sick and worn-out old woman."

I couldn't stop thinking of 'Boa's words. Sheer panic invaded my soul when I thought of being sent back to a FARC camp.

When I asked 'Jezid' what was going on, he confirmed my fears, "The Army's everywhere, especially on the road to Bogotá. I had ordas to walkya back to camp early tomorra morning, but with this change'a plans, we gonna wait 'til 'Boa' gives the word on Sunday morning."

Chapter 50

SEBASTIAN

Jezid told me he had instructions for us to eat at a FARC camp along the way. Immersed in my thoughts, I hardly noticed the basketball court next to an abandoned schoolhouse where we stopped. There were several tents and I could hear our captors yelling with the filthy language that was now so familiar to me. They had just finished their dinner and the woman on duty had left some rice and beans for us.

I noticed a sad-looking, bearded man in his late fifties. He had long hair and was not wearing a FARC uniform. He seemed anxious to strike up a conversation. The 'guerrilleros' were outside and we were left alone in the kitchen for about twenty minutes. His name was Sebastián. He told me I was the only kidnapped person he had met during the twenty-two months he had been held prisoner.

Sebastián told me the circumstances of his abduction. He was presiding a meeting at the Agricultural Association in his small city when the shooting began. One of his body-guards was killed, two were wounded, and in a matter of seconds he found himself in the trunk of a car. After a three hour drive they stopped and locked him up in the bathroom of a miserable shack, and kept him there for a month. He wasn't even allowed to walk, exercise, read, watch T.V. or spend any time in the fresh air.

The only 'furniture' available was a bathtub with a filthy mattress and his only chair was a toilet bowl without a lid. The only light came from a tiny 'window' without glass near the ceiling, with no net to keep the bats and insects out. For torture, they left the light on every night. His place of captivity was close to an airport and the unbearable noise of the frequent departures and landings was driving him crazy.

The only person Sebastián spoke with was a man who was trained to pressure, constantly, for information about his family and their properties. His main focus was to confuse Sebastian and put words in his mouth. This man and the woman who brought him his meals always wore head masks when they entered his 'room'.

After four nightmarish weeks, Sebastián was taken to a FARC camp where they kept him indefinitely. They told him right away that this was going to be a "very long economic retention". In twenty months he was moved five times; twice high up on the freezing mountain wilderness, and three times in the tropical jungle. Some of those camps were surrounded by poppy flower plantations. Poppy-seed is the raw material for heroine.

Because he was a rich man, Sebastián was never taken to a camp like ours and he was the only prisoner among his captors. His new living quarters were better than the bathroom where they kept him at first. He slept in the same area as the comandantes, on a wooden bed with a mattress. They had a generator for electricity, and a computer, which was only available to the FARC leaders, and a TV that he was sometimes allowed to watch.

Sebastián was considered 'hot merchandise' so occasionally they gave him a piece of chicken, an egg, and every so often, a fruit or vegetable. He told me they even gave him sleeping pills and medicine and if he was very ill, took him to the doctor at the main camp. There was no way he could have access to a piece of paper to write a note to his wife, so I memorized their phone number and promised to call her as soon as I reached civilization.

Even though Sebastián was not as undernourished and ragged as we were, his condition was even worse. I could imagine how it felt not to have a decent, trustworthy person to talk with.

"They are asking for an outrageous ransom, an amount my family will never be able to pay. I guess I'll have to rot here, among these beasts," he said.

When Jezid came to get me, Sebastian and I said our goodbyes, and promised to look each other up in Bogotá.

Chapter 51

FARC CHANGED THEIR PLANS

My sons had rented a big Jeep. First, they removed the paneling on the back doors, squeezed the money that had been packed in boxes into the empty space, and put the paneling back in place. They packed a few sacks of chicken feed in the trunk so Jaime and Julio could pass as local farmers, in case the police stopped them on the desolate road that would take them to the appointed destination. The officers in the area must have been aware that when one-time passengers were traveling those desolate roads, they were usually on their way to pay a ransom, which is illegal in Colombia. Nevertheless, they have learned to 'look the other way' so the kidnapped people might get their chance to return to safety.

On Saturday Jaime and Julio left Bogotá at eight a.m. They were going to meet 'Boa' at one p.m. for the 'transaction' and they had to be there on time. 'Boa', was constantly on the phone with David, as well as with Jezid. 'Boa's timing was totally unrealistic. He expected us to be there in five hours by foot, and it actually took us eleven hours, with the help of the horse that appeared out of the fog like a miracle.

David and 'Boa' had agreed they would send me home on Saturday, immediately after they counted the money. However, a new development changed things. 'Boa' told David the FARC had decided to count and collect the money on Saturday, but they weren't going to release me until Sunday.

David called Julio. He was upset and told him the discouraging news that the bandits had unexpectedly changed the game. The Comité asked for time to discuss what should be done. Shortly, they instructed Jaime and Julio to make a U-turn and return to Bogotá with the money, immediately. Thank God they were able to get away.

My family was unnerved when they returned without me that evening and Julio, who had managed the harrowing experience to perfection, was on the verge of a breakdown. It must have been difficult for my heroes to step into the Jeep and head out again the next morning—but God bless them, they did.

Chapter 52

AT THE FARM

AT ABOUT NINE thirty p.m. we reached a small, wooden house next to an empty, old farm house. Jezid helped me get off the horse. Carmen, the caretaker, was a peasant woman in her late fifties who lived there with her son and daughter. Like most land owners in Colombia, the 'patron' hadn't been there in several years.

After a heart-felt welcome, Carmen fixed me a bed where I was warm and comfortable for the first time in months, but I couldn't fall asleep. The idea of going back to one of those camps was tormenting me and I spent the worst, sleepless night of my life! Somehow, I held on and prayed the area was not being patrolled by the Army and the FARC would release me the next morning.

My bed was in a corner of the room where Pablo, a middle aged man also slept. When we were alone, Pablo told me he had been captured a week before in Chía, a town close to Bogotá. The FARC wasn't demanding any money from his family—there must have been something else they wanted from him; probably information about someone they were planning to kidnap. When he asked me to let him have my boots when I went free, I assured him he would get not only the boots, but also the FARC uniform I had on.

I got up very early on Sunday morning and looked forward to taking a shower in Carmen's bathroom. How marvelous it was to have some privacy, to lock myself in a real bathroom and use a toilet, a sink and a shower! Walls and doors were something to be taken for granted, until now. I certainly appreciated that little bathroom and its door. The cold water, coming from a shower fixture, was delightful. And there was even a towel! Who cared if it was clean or not? I wasn't particular about anything by now!

It was still dark when Jezid knocked on the door. He sounded quite enthusiastic and told me, "'Boa' gav 'me ordas to go ahead—we're clear'o 'vultures' and we'll keep on walkin'.

I put my dirty clothes back on and returned to the house. Jezid was trying to call 'Boa' for further instructions, but he couldn't get through. Finally, at about seven thirty, 'Boa' ordered him to walk me to the place where I was to be picked up. Jezid said, "Boa makes these jokes to scare 'ya old chuchos". In other words, his statement about the 'vultures' was nothing more than a sadistic show of power to frighten me.

Jezid told me to get ready for the 'three-hour walk', we were leaving very soon. I asked Pablo to come with us so he would be sure to get my boots and uniform. Pablo wasn't considered 'merchandise' but a fountain of valuable information, so even though he was always guarded, he had some degree of freedom. Carmen served us breakfast, and we left.

After about two hours of walking, Jezid's phone rang. It was 'Boa', ordering him to take me back to Carmen's house—they were having problems and I would not be released. I was stunned and speechless. We turned around and walked in silence.

We were not far from the little wooden house, when Jezid's phone rang again. It was 'Boa' telling him to hurry back; they were sending me home! Pablo and I followed Jezid until we reached a narrow winding, mountain road. The air was getting warmer than anywhere else I had been in the last five months.

Everybody in the area was wearing a FARC uniform. I saw about eight abandoned cars that had been set on fire along the roadside. They must have been robbed from other kidnapped people and I wondered if my Peugeot truck was among them. This God forsaken road must have been a 'no man´s land' between FARC territory and the free world.

Chapter 53

WHERE'S THE MONEY?

MEANWHILE, EARLY ON Sunday morning my dear Jaime and Julio, started out again to complete the 'transaction'. The 'Comité' was in session and David called Julio often to find out if everything was O.K. The level of tension was sky high.

Jaime had been driving fast for approximately three hours when they were intercepted. Three men jumped out of a parked truck. One of them identified himself as 'Boa'.

He asked, "Did ya bring the money?"

"Yes", answered Jaime, "We have the money, but where is Mrs. Myriam?"

'Boa' suddenly became friendly and invited Jaime and Julio to drive to the camp and have a few drinks with him. Jaime told 'Boa' that he couldn't drink any liquor because it was not compatible with the medicine he was taking. Also, they needed to take Mrs. Myriam back to Bogotá as soon as possible.

'Boa' was in a good mood that day and they agreed to count the money together. Julio opened the back door of the Jeep and took out the paneling where the packets of fifty-thousand peso bills were stacked. They got the money out of the car and carried it to 'Boa's truck where they started counting.

In the meantime, Jaime jumped back in and took off with two 'guerilleros', who instructed him where to go, on the road where I was being escorted by the two 'muchachos'.

*   *   *   *   *   *

Jezid, Pablo and I, had been walking on the curvy, dirt road for about three hours when a grey Jeep came into view. When I saw who was driving, my heart skipped a beat. I started running to the car. It was my very dear nephew, Jaime! He signaled me to stay calm, but how could I stay calm and control such joy?

When the 'guerrilleros' stepped out of the Jeep, I immediately climbed in front, took off my boots and the FARC uniform I had been wearing over my sweat suit, and rapidly handed them to Pablo. I waved good-bye while Jaime drove away as fast as he could.

We drove rapidly back to the place where Julio and 'Boa' were counting the money, and Julio jumped in the back. We were off in a few seconds!

Chapter 54

BACK TO FREEDOM!

It was 3:45 on that glorious Sunday afternoon and I had a hard time believing that this time, I was truly on my way to freedom! Julio put me on the phone with my sons, but our tears and excitement didn't allow us to speak.

About thirty minutes later, when he was sure we were out of FARC territory and the tension had decreased somewhat, Jaime stopped the Jeep so we could catch our breath and relax. We stepped out and the three of us stood on the road in a tight embrace and cried.

Ricardo and his wife had sent me some clothes in case I wanted to change. But all I wanted was to get out of there as fast as possible. They also sent me a chicken sandwich and a can of Coca Cola. I couldn't believe it! Nothing had ever tasted so wonderful. Nevertheless, after two bites of the sandwich and three sips of the beverage, I was full.

I talked and talked. My appearance and what I said must have touched the hearts of my heroes. The delight was beyond words. Julio put me on the phone with my sons again and this time, I was able to express my love to them.

The road was deserted and we only came across two cars during the whole ride. After about three hours of fast driving along the mountain road,

I saw the first lights of the city in the far horizon. They grew bigger and brighter the closer we came to Bogotá. To me, they were lights of hope and happiness.

We reached a disorderly neighborhood on the outskirts of the city full of houses, cars, trucks, buses and people out on the streets. The variety of colors the people were wearing; reds, whites, yellows, greens and blues, and the city noise, with cars beeping and people yelling, were so exhilarating! I was especially overjoyed to see children and dogs again. There was liveliness everywhere. It was marvelous to be in the middle of that chaotic traffic, so typical of Bogotá.

Jaime and Julio were amazed to watch the spell that came over me as I became enchanted by such simple, everyday happenings that were extraordinary to me at that moment. I felt as if I was landing on planet earth for the first time. It took almost two hours to cross the city from southwest to northeast. As we got closer to home, everything was becoming familiar. We passed a group of Government buildings, a hospital, a shopping area, an amusement park; my school, the National Park, my neighborhood, my bank, my favorite supermarket, and finally, we drove into the garage of the building where I lived.

When the doorman recognized me, he embraced me and burst out crying—so did two friends from the building I met in the elevator. Seconds later, I was in the arms of my beloved sons and of course, my Mutti. Being together again was glorious!!! Nevertheless, I could see on their faces the strain of the previous months. But now the hellish ordeal was over! They were relieved to see that even though I looked and smelled miserable, my mind seemed to be O.K.

Jaime and Julio stayed for dinner and we all thanked God with a very emotional prayer. They shared details of their last two days, and it was obvious it had been intense and nerve-wrecking.

My sons and I talked until three in the morning. I was surrounded by so much love. At last, I dozed off in the safety of my home, but not before taking a hot bubble-bath while listening to my favorite, Chopin piano concert, and putting on my clean, soft pink cotton-velour pajamas.

Chapter 55

BORN AGAIN

THE NEXT MORNING my sons pampered me with breakfast in bed, like we used to have on Sundays when they were children. They cuddled me, and we laughed and cried with tears of joy. They had prepared a beautiful platter with all of my favorite tropical fruits. A few hours later, when word spread that I had been freed, my apartment began to fill up with flower arrangements sent by friends to welcome me.

Doris called my stylist who came to do my hair and hands. The whole top of my head had turned white and the old, faded brown, unruly hair, straggled around my face after my first shampoo in five months. We had to decide whether I should dye it, or leave it white. I asked my stylist to color my eyebrows, cut off as much of the old, dyed hair as possible, and apply a rinse for the time being.

My sons advised me to leave the country and spend some time with Alejandro and his family in the United States. Since Alejandro is a Psychiatrist, his loving care and professionalism was just what I needed. We all knew it wasn't safe for me to stay in Bogotá. The FARC usually keep calling, "just to say hello." Alejandro had already booked my plane ticket along with his own for the following Thursday. Nevertheless, the final decision was mine.

Early Monday morning I called the families of my kidnapped companions. The first person I talked to was Victor's wife, Liliana. She told me she would travel to visit me in Bogotá early the next day.

Then I called Augusto's wife, Claudia, who came immediately. From what he had told me, I knew Claudia was a very special person. Her husband's kidnapping had affected her deeply. She was so thin, she looked like she had been kidnapped herself. David advised her not to enter into negotiations with the FARC by herself, but it was too late. She had already reached an agreement and it took her three additional weeks and many terrible hardships to get Augusto back to freedom. The FARC negotiators are known to be meaner to women than they are to men.

I spent that joyous Monday with my family. My grand-children were frightened by my appearance, but after a while they were as cheerful and loving as always. Embracing them fulfilled the heavenly moments I had been looking forward to for so long. My brother Martin, my dear sister-in-law, my daughters-in-law, my niece and nephew came in the morning. Everyone was delighted that the nightmare was over.

I called Sebastián's wife in Manizales, whose number I had recently memorized, and told her about my short visit with her husband. This was the only first-hand news she ever heard about Sebastián in the twenty-two months he was kidnapped. She said his family was ready to pay the ransom and hopefully, they would have Sebastian back very soon.

My sons invited the members of the Comité and their spouses for dinner on Monday at a nearby restaurant. It was a lovely celebration. The happy ending to this gruesome episode brought closure and relief to all of us. I was still very weak, but being able to thank these amazing people, in person, who were responsible for my freedom, gave me the strength to express my gratitude with all my heart.

When Liliana, Victor's wife, came to visit me on Tuesday morning, my sons strongly advised her to engage a tough lawyer to negotiate Victor's freedom. Fourteen months had passed since he was captured, and all their money was draining away. Liliana was obviously deeply distressed, and the bandits were taking advantage of her fragile condition with their second demand.

The next morning, the relatives of my other kidnapped friends came to visit. It obviously meant a lot to them to hear first-hand news about their loved ones. Three of Panchita's daughters and her son felt somewhat relieved when I told them she was in good spirits and had most of us working-out every morning.

Franco's son came with Teresa's brother. I advised Esperanza's sisters to be patient—this was a matter of time and money. I didn't tell Gunther's wife and daughter how depressed he was. Just knowing that he was alive was a blessing to them. The bandits hadn't called them, not even to demand a ransom.

On Wednesday, Alejandro took me to the dentist. When he saw the huge hole in my molar he told me how fortunate it was that years earlier, I had a root canal treatment. Otherwise, even a drink of water would have been excruciating.

My cardiologist found me in reasonably good condition. He said it was a miracle I had stayed healthy without my blood pressure medicine over such a long period of time. He ordered a series of tests which were performed the next day and the results were OK.

I spent the rest of the day with Mutti and the children. She was disappointed that I would leave with Alejandro, but she understood that for my safety, I needed to leave the country.

My sons invited my friends to a welcome-home party on Tuesday evening.

Chapter 56

FOLLOW-UP ON MY COMPANIONS

Now THAT MOST of my companions are free, some of us have been able to visit each other in Bogotá. I often see Federico, Augusto, and their wives. We don't talk about our ordeal and our meetings are full of warmth and affection. We went through so much together, and I have many reasons to be eternally grateful for their friendship. I have also seen Blanca and Esperanza a few times.

*   *   *   *   *   *

Augusto's wife, Claudia, had to sell their house and even their car to pay his ransom. They hope to migrate to Canada. Claudia told me that she had the help of a neighbor to negotiate. Since everyone in their family was young, she only had a small financial contribution from a member of her family.

*   *   *   *   *   *

Blanca is home with her family and her 'papito'. They are still struggling to keep up with the payments he "owes the FARC". They always call a week before a payment is due, and her family is constantly being threatened 'just in case they don't come through with the payment'.

*   *   *   *   *   *

Esperanza was sent home two weeks after my release to collect a huge sum for Armando's ransom. It took her five more months and three trips to the 'páramo' to negotiate personally with 'Romaña', the comandante in charge of their case. The demand was outrageous and she had no help from Armando's family.

*   *   *   *   *   *

I called my friend Carlos, our elderly companion, who was sent out by himself into the wilderness because he didn't have anybody who could pay his ransom. His daughter told me she knew that Carlos had been released, but she never heard a word from him, and he never reached home. It was so sad to hear this; he had been a good friend and I thought very highly of him.

*   *   *   *   *   *

When I saw Federico and his wife Gloria, I inquired about their engineering company. Gloria took leave from her job at an insurance company and took over Federico's office. No wonder Federico always said, "I'm in good hands, my wife has great judgment."

*   *   *   *   *   *

When I called Manuel, one of his brothers told me that he left the country with his family.

*   *   *   *   *   *

Panchita and most of her family went to live in Panama. Shortly after they left, the FARC kidnapped her daughter who had visited me in Bogotá. Another one of her daughters, a lawyer, stayed in Colombia to negotiate her freedom. When I called Panchita a few months later, she told me the FARC had murdered her daughter, Sandra, who was abducted after Panchita was released.

*   *   *   *   *   *

Three months after I returned, the FARC finally released Victor, but not before Liliana paid a second, very high sum. They were left in bankruptcy.

*   *   *   *   *   *

I always had a sad feeling about Franco. On one of my trips back to Colombia, a year after my release, I called him again. His son told me they were still trying to negotiate his ransom, but the FARC never provided proof of life which was most discouraging.

*   *   *   *   *   *

Some people need a long time to recover their emotional stability—others never do. They are usually depressed, irritable, unpredictable and very different from their normal selves—sometimes emotionally crippled for life. It is common to have nightmares, negative fantasies and paranoia or to suffer from Post Traumatic Shock Syndrome. They frequently have to deal with conflicts, disloyalties and other unpleasant surprises that arise in most families during their absence, especially when so much money is involved. And divorce is frequent.

A hostage, usually a young woman who is vulnerable and in need of affection, may fall in love or become infatuated with one of her captors when treated with a little kindness and compassion. This feeling is called the 'Stockholm Syndrome'. Heiress Patty Hearst became an accomplice to her captors when she was kidnapped by the Symbionese Liberation Army in California, 1974.

A very young Colombian girl also fell victim to the Stockholm Syndrome. When, after a year of captivity she was finally released, she left the country, pregnant with the child of a 'guerrillero'.

Chapter 57

MY HEALING PROCESS

My inner healing began while staying with my sons' families in the United States for three months. I then returned to Bogotá to spend time with Mutti and put my house in order. This meant sorting out personal belongings and packing things in boxes. My favorite objects were put in a storage center—the others were sent to charities or given away.

On my return to Bogotá, a neighbor who lived next to 'Buganviles' called to ask about our plans for the farm. She told me someone in their family would be interested in buying it, if the price was reasonable. Of course we decided to sell and I assured her the price would be very low. Eventually, her brother bought "Buganviles" under the condition that we remove all the people who worked there as soon as possible. She said they had reason to believe that one of them was the informant.

To end a worker's contract, Colombian law entitles employees to a lump sum called "Despido sin Justa Causa" (Unjust dismissal). Our caretakers and the other worker had been employed at 'Buganviles' for eighteen years, which meant they were entitled to a sum that was almost the equivalent of the amount we received for the farm.

I never returned to Buganviles, not even to pick up items that were important to me. The new owner probably threw away my swimming trophies, some of my photo albums and my hat collection. I promised my sons I would never call to find out.

*   *   *   *   *   *

My kidnapping marked a clear 'before – after' change in my life. Things could never go back to the way they were. My grandchildren are growing up fast and I am privileged to accompany them throughout these formative years. When I am tempted to complain, I make it a point to remember that my life was once so much worse.

I'm very proud of my sons and grateful to them. Despite the pressure, they held together and stayed strong to support me. They knew how important it was to be united during these difficult times. I also thank God for their wonderful wives. Each one had the patience and generosity to make the necessary sacrifices, and offered their husband's moral support, love and understanding.

David's strength of spirit enabled him to head up the negotiation in an intelligent and tactful manner despite his adversary's hostility and disdain. It is understandable that David never wanted to talk about anything related to the FARC or to kidnappings again.

It must have been difficult for Clarita, David's wife, to stay alone while he was far away. She took full responsibility of their small children and their home, while David stayed in Bogotá, struggling with 'Boa' to save my life. I love her and appreciate her cooperation and patience.

After David's tasks were finished, Alejandro took me under his wing. Four days after my release, we traveled to his home. When his wife, Martha, and their children came to greet us at the airport, Marcela, their four year-old, noticed right away how much my appearance had changed. She told me in her most polite manner,

"Omi, you will go to Heaven very soon."

With long hours of therapeutic care during the two months I stayed at their home, my son Alejandro, my private and loving Psychiatrist, patiently put together all the bits and pieces of my injured psyche.

I avoid overstaying my visit in anybody's home. Because this was such a long stay, I was touched by Martha's efforts to make me feel welcome. I love her and thank her for her warmth and sense of humor, which contributed greatly to my recovery.

Ricardo and Doris, who had traveled so many hours every week-end to Bogotà during the time of my captivity, demonstrated their joy to have me back. Doris, who is also the daughter of one of my long-time friends, has always, since she was a child, been especially dear to me.

Each of my sons paid his part towards the ransom, and I was told from the beginning not to ask how much it was—they had agreed never to tell me.

My dear Mutti also contributed generously, and despite her poor health and old age of ninety two, she held on to life until I returned. My reencounter with her gave us long hours to talk and we became closer than we had ever been before. We reconnected in a profound way. I am grateful that when her time came, she died peacefully, four months after my release.

Chapter 58

THE NEW ME

I USED TO be what in Colombian colloquial language you would call 'una señora bien'—a classy lady of high principles. She is part of a well to do family, carries out her role as a loving mother to perfection, and is usually the wife of a successful man. She has a clean past and is accustomed to a comfortable life. She is spiritual, helpful and warm hearted, and careful never to offend anyone. She volunteers for charitable work and enjoys a busy social schedule of dinners, art exhibits, and theater.

She reads a lot and keeps herself well informed, does not smoke and only indulges in a drink or two at social events. She dresses and behaves impeccably for every occasion. She will successfully take on the direction of her family whenever it`s necessary and is well liked and respected in her social group. She keeps herself fit and attractive by exercising and visiting the beauty parlor for special occasions.

After my kidnapping, I lived by myself in a small apartment in Florida and became fond of my new, independent lifestyle. I quickly learned that if I failed to pick something up, it would stay exactly where I left it. Unless I washed them, the dishes stayed dirty in the sink. María, who was my loyal worker for

24 years, wasn't there to pick up after me. If I wanted to wear a freshly ironed dress, or sleep in ironed sheets, I had to iron them myself or take them to the cleaner.

Instead of being dropped off and picked up at the front door of a store by my driver, I was obliged to find my own parking space. It took many crucial and distressful minutes to acquire the habit of remembering where I parked my car. Filling my gas tank became a normal task.

When I had an appetite for "Ajiaco", (a typical Colombian soup) or "Wiener Schnitzel" that María prepared regularly for small groups of guests, I had to buy the ingredients myself and get to work. My everyday meals were healthy and simple, mostly salads and fruits, and a few frozen dinners I always kept in the freezer.

I was lucky to be living in the same city, Boca Raton, as David's family which gave me a chance to enjoy them frequently. Part of the time he ran his business in Bogota online and by phone. My other grandchildren stayed with me on vacations and I was fortunate that my cousins from Vienna lived close by. Of course I missed my friends in Bogotá, but I was blessed with several new, refreshing friendships.

I became more self-reliant, and learned to consult my map and compass whenever I was lost rather than depending blindly on others. The beautiful city I lived in, so generous in parks and golf courses, wasn't easy to navigate. Sometimes, when driving at 80 miles per hour on a freeway, a question arose: IS THIS REALLY ME?

One of the things I admire about the American lifestyle is the youthful attitude of its older citizens. They seem to be younger than their counterparts elsewhere. The generation before mine still leads a good life, putting their mental and emotional faculties to good use until the last day of their lives.

My activities included weekly meetings at a writers' workshop with a delightful group of new friends. They were very supportive and I learned much from their writings and critiques. I attended the amusing Storytelling Camp's three day meetings several times. Water aerobics became my favorite sport. I played cards weekly with a group of friends and walked about two miles every day with a neighbor.

Joining the Toastmasters Club was a life-changing experience. It is hard to believe that any of the toastmasters were ever shy at their beginning stages. One of my activities was volunteering as an interpreter at the hospital for Spanish-speaking migrants. These activities were not only educational but important to my healing process, along with writing this memoir.

How I loved the tiny brown sparrows that sat by the hundreds on the telephone wires after the rain. It's remarkable to watch them move over so quickly to make space for the arriving flocks. And then there was a lovely duck couple that lived with their six ducklings by the small lake outside my window. They waddled over every day for their mid-morning snack. These small, but meaningful events filled my heart with joy.

CONCLUSION

Being kidnapped transformed every one of us captives in a different way. In the conversations we held after our release, most of us agreed that we had been spiritually strengthened. We were physically inactive most of the time, which obliged us to focus our energy on survival. We learned to depend on God, and the comfort of prayer became a vital part of our daily lives. In my case, I attribute my reasonably stable emotional health during the experience to the wonderful group of people I was fortunate to have as fellow hostages. I have read about other groups of hostages who spent their captivity of six, ten, and even 14 years, fighting amongst themselves. In some cases the other abducted victims became their enemies and they ended up feeling closer to their kidnappers.

Being kidnapped is subhuman and denigrating. Every person reacts differently to such atrocities and humiliations. People in captivity are labeled with an imaginary price tag. Being forced to live under these conditions reduces the victims to a category of valuable, but neglected animals. It is disgraceful that a person can only be spared when the ransom is paid. There is no respect for corporal intimacy or personal choices, which are often discussed publicly and ridiculed.

You must stock up much courage to face the hurt and humiliation of being laughed at when you pray, fall, cry, and even when you are sick. Having to satisfy your physical needs and bathe in the presence of others, dress in their uniforms, eat their disgusting food, and be deprived of some of the basic personal hygiene and minimal medical attention, is an assault to one's dignity. Aside from the cold and the mud, profound anxiety is magnified by not knowing how long the torture will last. The main duty that a kidnapped person owes to his family is to stay out of trouble and try to survive.

The healing process was long and arduous. Yet, those of us who were lucky enough to overcome the suffering discovered a new and much less complicated way of life. I now find pleasure in the simplest things and often find myself thanking God for the many blessings that I used to take for granted in everyday life.

Things like enjoying the love of my wonderful family, sharing good and bad experiences with special friends, being treated with courtesy, listening to beautiful music, sleeping in a bed, using a toilet, taking a warm shower, eating a healthy meal, reading a good book and watching TV have become invaluable priorities. Also, enjoying privacy, or simply having freedom of choice, are things I don't take for granted anymore. Many trivialities that were once important have completely lost their value. Just having my life back is much more important than the whereabouts of the lovely things that held sentimental value. At times, some item I was particularly fond of comes to mind, but somehow, the attachment is not the same.

I am now living alone in a small house with a pretty little garden and my cat, Michín. As time goes by and this experience is left behind, I continue to gather the information life has brought my way. The image I upheld for so many years holds little importance to me now, after having struggled for sheer survival in the midst of impossible conditions where all that mattered to pull me through was inner character and faith in a Superior Force.

Life has a way of bringing along surprises born from suffering and pain. Instead of remembering only the dark side of the kidnapping ordeal, I choose to hold onto a spirit of cheerfulness, accentuated by the fact that I can still laugh at a joke, enjoy my family and friends, and am able to share my story. It's only a dot in the big picture, a grain of sand by the ocean, but I hope to pass on not only the trauma of my kidnapping, but the lessons gleaned from it.

If my words can communicate hope to those who are presently passing through a precarious situation, then there has been a purpose for it all. Never give up hope, never give in to fear, hold on and the light will appear even in the darkest hour.

The most devastating experience of my life occurred a few years after my liberation when my beloved son, David, who saved my life, suddenly passed away from a heart attack at the age of forty six. I struggle with the unanswered question, "Why did God take him, and not me?" Only someone who has lost a son or daughter can know how it feels. As terrible as the kidnapping was, it can't compare to this kind of grief. I start to miss David every morning at 6:30, when he would call me on his way to the office. Believing someone so dear to my heart is waiting for me on the other side, makes his absence a bit more bearable.

THE END

A SPECIAL TRIBUTE TO MY BELOVED SON DAVID

By far the most devastating experience of my life occurred five years after my liberation when David, who worked so tirelessly to achieve my freedom and saved my life, suddenly passed away from a heart attack at the age of forty-six.

I struggle with the unanswered question, "Why did God take him, and not me?" Only someone who has lost a son or daughter can know how this feels. As terrible as the kidnapping was, it can't compare to this kind of grief. I start to miss David every morning at 6:30, when he would call me on his way to the office.

Believing someone so dear to my heart is waiting for me on the other side, makes his absence a bit more bearable.

EPILOGUE

PERISHED PEACE PROCESS
Where we are in the early 21ˢᵗ Century
What we may hope for
BY GENERAL ALVARO VALENCIA TOVAR

By the late 1990's, it became evident that the FARC terrorists were increasing the intensity of their aggression against their helpless, fellow citizens. Three Irish terrorist mercenaries from the IRA (Irish Republican Army) were arrested by Colombian authorities after spending five weeks in the "Zona de Distension" training FARC soldiers in the manufacture and use of bombs and other terrorist weapons, especially in the use of an explosive called Semtex H, produced in the Czech Republic, which is strong enough to blow up modern, fortified buildings. This training prepared the "FARC Street Militia" for urban warfare and they began to extend their brutal attacks into the big cities.

This training made the FARC even more cruel and audacious. They even attempted to blow up the dam surrounding the reservoir that supplies Bogotá with water. Thank God, this and many other attempts were unsuccessful, but who knows what comes next. If they had succeeded, a small city near the reservoir would have been buried in mud, and Bogotá's population of seven million people would have been left without water.

Local news showed the FARC using live dogs wearing explosive collars, tied up in key places where people they wanted to murder would inevitably pass by. During his campaign, Doctor Alvaro Uribe Velez, our President Elect at that time, had four close calls. One of them was a bomb attached to a donkey standing on the roadside where he passed in his car.

The four years of fruitless President Pastrana-FARC peace talks, served one purpose. Other countries became aware, through foreign representatives who personally attended the talks, that the FARC terrorists were not at all interested in making peace. Their main interest was to keep their "Safe Haven" just the way it was, while they take over the rest of the country.

On February 20, 2002, an agreement was signed between government representatives and the FARC chieftains in the presence of the Ambassadors from "ten friendly countries" and a Catholic Bishop. The agreement was to sign a planned chronogram that would gradually de-escalate the intensity of the armed conflict, arriving at an indefinite truce to be reached on April 7.

On the same day this agreement was signed, the FARC launched a brutal terrorist offensive. Bridges, electrical plants, oil pipes, and cargo trucks were blown up all over the country. There were massive kidnappings, including one female Presidential candidate; several small villages were destroyed, FARC style, with gas cylinder explosions.

Of course, the timetable for the proposed truce failed. The FARC representatives at the negotiating table found excuse after excuse not to comply, while terrorist offensives continued on with renewed fury. An unfortunate incident finally brought the dying peace process to its end. The FARC force-landed, and abandoned a passenger plane on an isolated road. They kidnapped a Senator on board. Twelve Congressmen and the

Governor of Antioquia were taken into captivity and later, eleven of them were assassinated.

That was the straw that broke the camel's back! That same evening, President Pastrana spoke to the nation on television, officially declaring the Peace Process closed. This took place at nine o'clock that night. At midnight the Armed Forces were to recover the Demilitarized Zone. The President formally accused the FARC, and specifically their leader, Tirofijo, of having deceived his Government and betraying their word.

In the midst of this tragedy, while the Government was striving for peace, the FARC manipulated the dialogues, using them as a springboard to launch their revolutionary purposes. The very social fabric of our society is being brutally torn apart by the alliance of armed gangs that used to be political guerrillas, and are now headed by leaders who lavishly finance their purchase of destructive hardware with drug money. The question arises: Is there any hope left for Colombia? May we find a little light at the end of the somber tunnel ahead?

I do believe the answers to these and many other questions of this kind are positive. Liberty, as Benjamin Franklin said, is a trembling light, for which many human beings have died in obscurity. Love for freedom has been a historic constant since the early days of the Colombian Republic, born from the oppression of Spanish dominion. Keeping that little light alive under the fury of the hurricane is what will save this wonderful country.

Democracy possesses hidden reserves that bring out enormous energy in times of anguishing crisis. These moral forces were tested during the 2002 elections when the Colombians massively voted for the former President Elect, Dr. Alvaro Uribe Velez. People dared to approach the voting urns under lethal threats from the FARC, who made every effort to sabotage the polls.

President Alvaro Uribe was a leader and statesman who understood in depth the precarious national situation and proposed reasonable solutions to the complex problems that confronted the Nation. What he said and did since the aftermath of the elections ushered in new hope.

Parallel to the implementation of a National Policy of Democratic Security with the enthusiastic cooperation of the Colombian citizens, the General Command of the Military Forces devised a sound strategy to meet the non-conventional warfare being conducted by the FARC and ELN. Information began to flow in the rural areas which allowed the combat intelligence to make continuous progress. Hard blows were inflicted to the narco-guerrillas and drug dealing elements.

Periodical surveys conducted by both Colombian and foreign experienced firms proved that between 70 and 80 percent of the people expressed their support and acceptance of President Alvaro Uribe and approved his performance. The goal to recover territory under the influence of FARC had by then reached astonishing results. Road traffic was no longer under the frightful menace of kidnapping and criminal assaults. Every town, even the smallest and more distance from the province capitals had recovered its civilian and police authorities.

Attacks to small, defenseless towns, with gas cylinders filled with pieces of metal, infectious materials and explosives, became only a nightmare of the past. Kidnapping decreased rapidly. The national economy flourished. The industrial expansion, foreign and national investments were quite noticeable and exports grew considerably. Many intellectuals, writers and newspaper columnists spoke of the post-conflict. The military called it post victory.

Written By General Valencia In July, 2011

President Uribe's second term in office ended on August 7, 2010. Juan Manuel Santos, who was his Minister of National Defense during his second term, won the polls by an impressive land slide election, which proved the acceptance of a clear majority of Colombians to the National Security Policy developed by President Uribe.

The continuity of policies assured by the Santos Presidency has been so far quite convenient for dealing with the rural violence. Knowing well the depth of the intricate situation, President Santos has made good use of the experience obtained during his successful association with President Uribe. Although the remains of FARC and ELN guerrillas still carry out isolated efforts to show that they are still alive, their criminal behavior has decreased to a point where they are not any longer a threat to political and social stability. Best of all, they have entirely lost any public backing and external recognition as they used to enjoy under their disguise as freedom fighters.

Colombia has improved consistently in terms of worldwide recognition as a true, democratic State. The American community is well aware of this nation's enormous contribution to peace and order, as well as to the preservation of human rights and International humanitarian law. There is, of course, a long road ahead to return to the full internal peace and restoration of human values that have suffered deep damage throughout the long internal turmoil. But the light at the end of the tunnel of darkness and suffering is clearing out forever.

WORDS FROM A FRIEND

Between the time Myriam was kidnapped and before her book was published, positive changes occurred on the Colombian front. The coast is not entirely clear yet, but there is a period of hope and renewal; freedom to travel around the country, prosper commercially and live in relative safety, was ushered in by the double term of President Alvaro Uribe. Understanding the desperate state of his country that has been a nesting place for terrorist groups and drug traffic for over five decades, he upheld a solid military stance and empowered the Army to advance against them, contrary to the defensive position adopted by former Colombian leaders. He established strong security measures all over the country and openly challenged the rebels, driving them back.

The original FARC leader, Tirofijo, author of the FARC movement, died a natural death. Raul Reyes and Mono Jojoy, the military and strategic leaders, as well as Alfonso Cano, the first commander who replaced Tirofijo, and several other high ranking FARC elements, were killed by the National Army.

After ten years of government military advances, the FARC guerrillas have been greatly weakened. Kidnapping is still prevalent and there are some victims under their claws.

It's clear that the complicated and long term political conflicts in Colombia cannot be solved in only a few years. The Colombian Government has maintained a conservative position, contrary to other Latin American countries, largely because there is no way to reason with the rebel movements, who insist on using violence and destruction to accomplish their goal—to take over the country at all cost. Colombia's narco-guerillas will do everything in their power not to lose control over the drug industry and the prosperity this has allowed them. In other words, no other Latin American country has suffered to the same extent, nor been obliged to seek outside help and use military force to this degree to protect its citizens. It has become necessary for Colombia's leaders to uphold a firm position, so as not to lose the progress and freedom gained over the last years. It is unfortunate that the Colombian government must spend so much money, time and energy fending off the furious aggressions of the FARC instead of using all of their resources to care for the people and reach out to the socially disadvantaged. Hopefully, there will be a time when the internal war will give way to peace and healing, bringing Colombia out of her "dark age" of violence and terrorism, once and for all.

Myriam began her book several years ago but was interrupted by the passing away of her eldest son, David, who suddenly died of a heart attack. He was the master-mind behind the negotiation for her freedom. Myriam's grief deeply affected her, rendering her incapable of continuing with her story. Now she has courageously taken it up once again, determined to be a 'voice in the desert' denouncing the injustice and horror of these attacks on basic, human rights.

Coming from a family who had to flee Hitler's Nazi regime, whose destiny was totally transformed by their immigration to Colombia, and who struggled to adapt in a new and challenging situation, has obviously granted Myriam with the innate capacity to overcome extreme situations.

Myriam's story is a tribute to personal liberty and cries out to the world to leave behind the cruel and primitive methods of control and imposition motivated by political or financial goals. It teaches valuable lessons on inner strength, love and survival, and the ability to overcome trauma by embracing what is true and vastly more important in life than material possessions in order to obtain ongoing, inner peace. If anyone has a right to speak of freedom in the face of unjustified captivity, it's Myriam.

A Friend